Copyright© 2020 Adult Coloring Book
By Trippy Art Publishing,
All rights reserved.

Stoners
Coloring Book For Adults

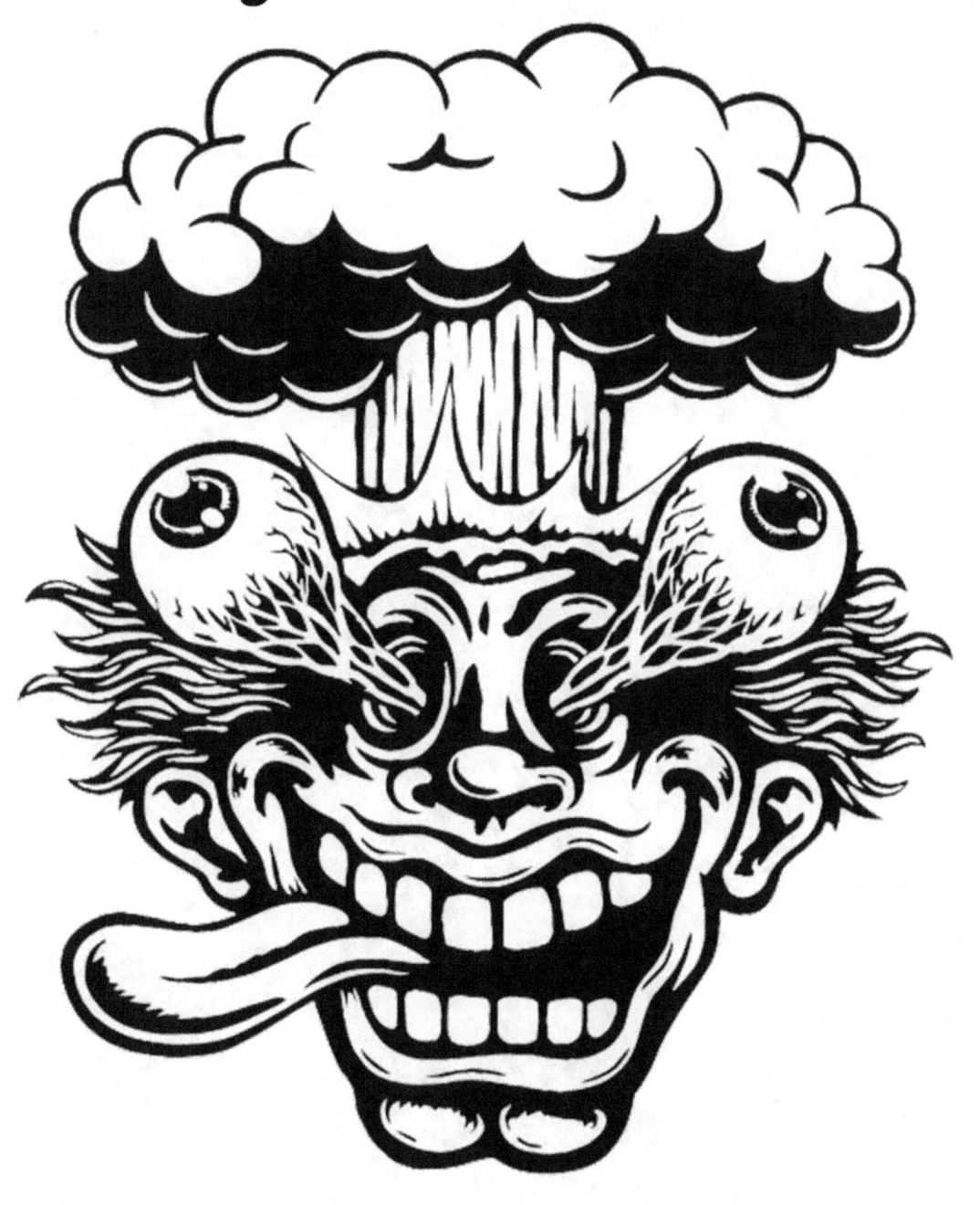

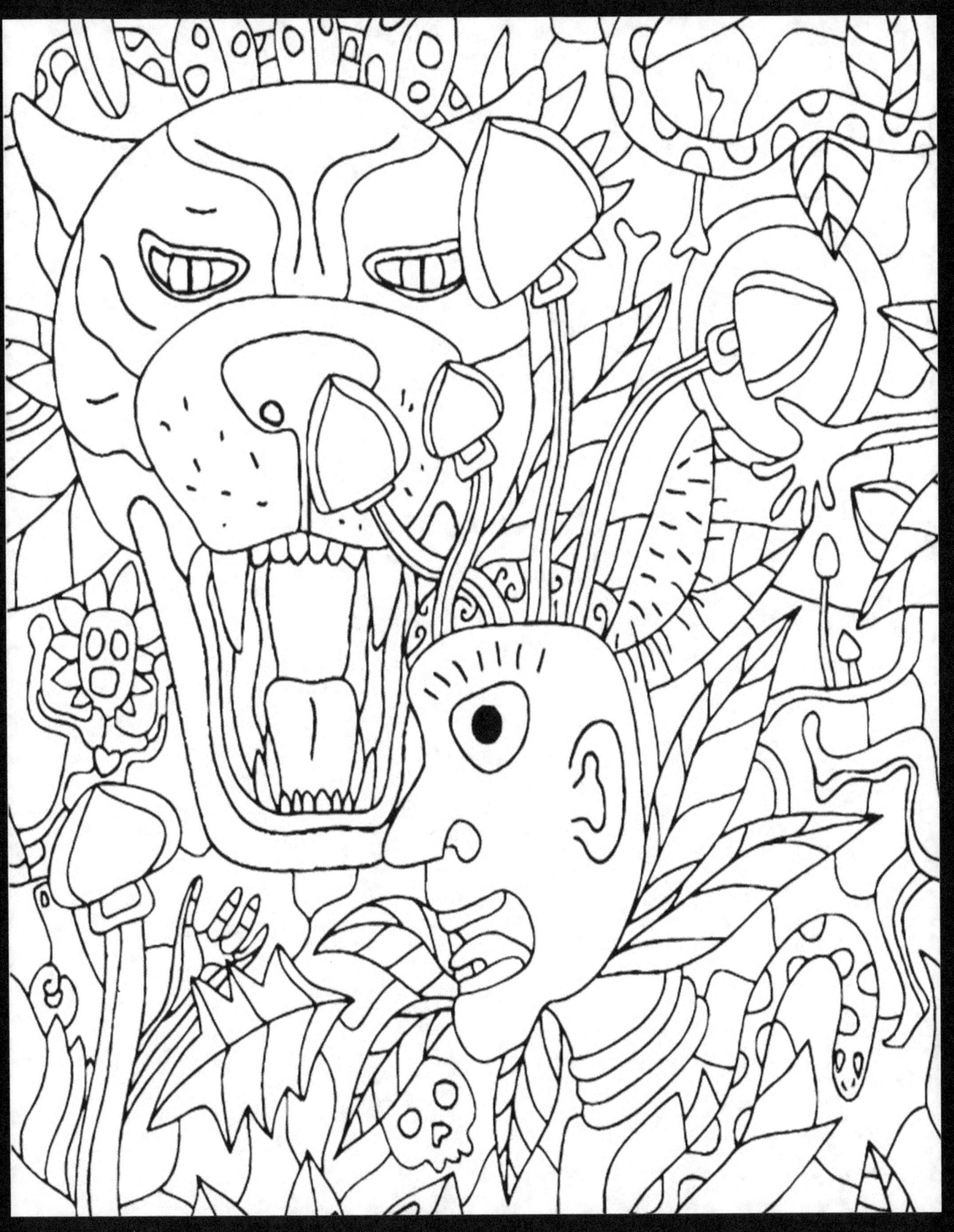

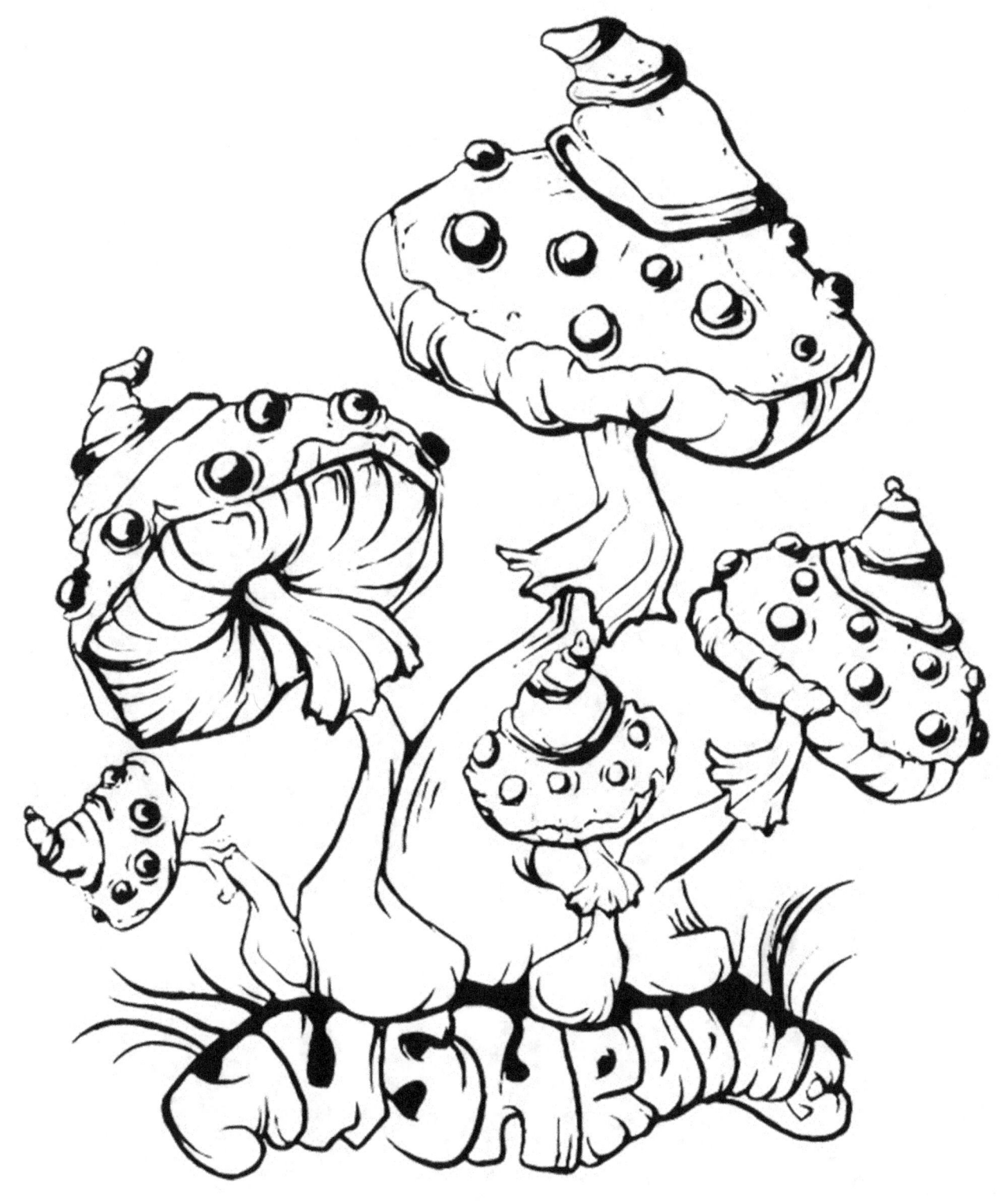

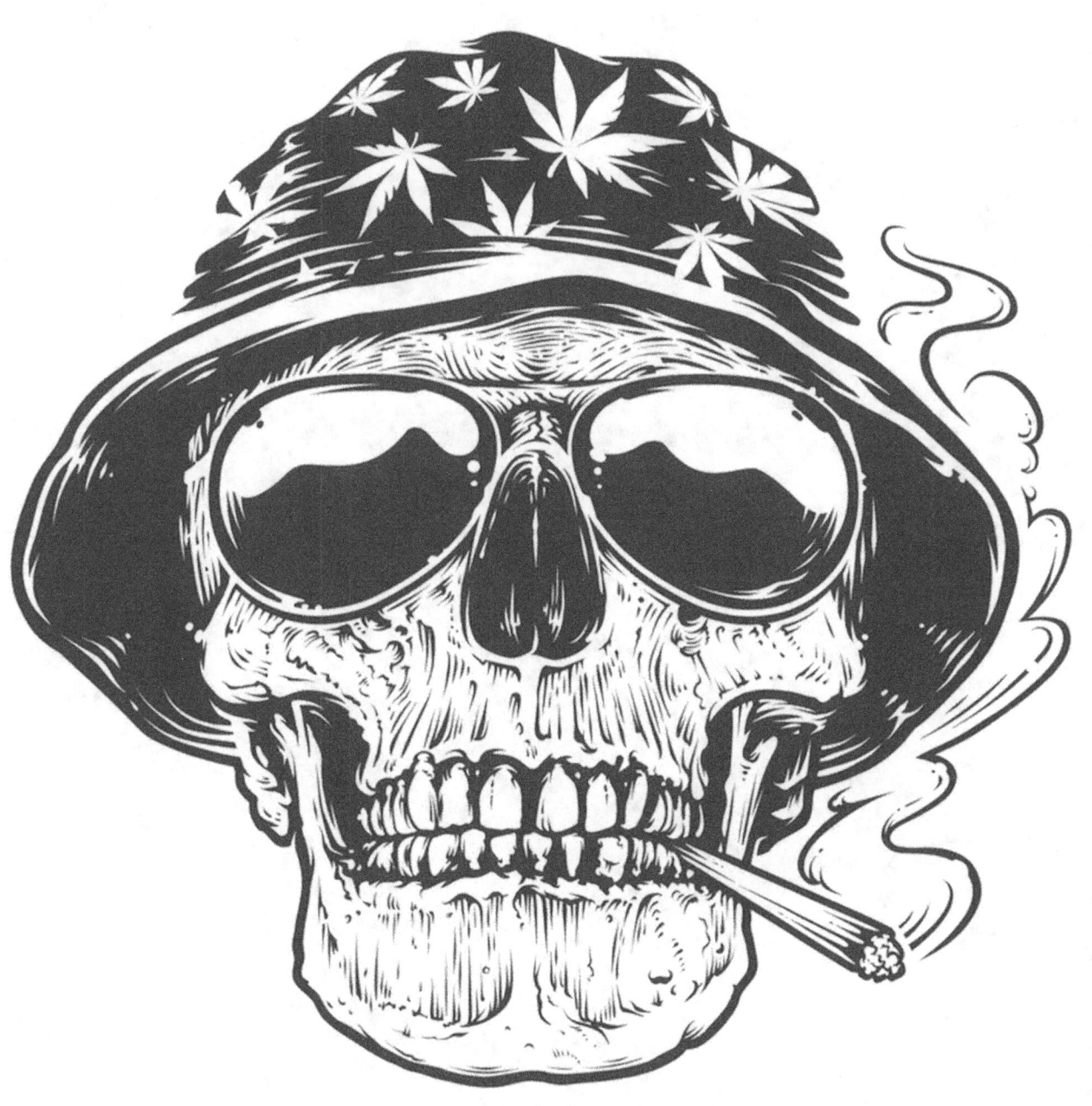

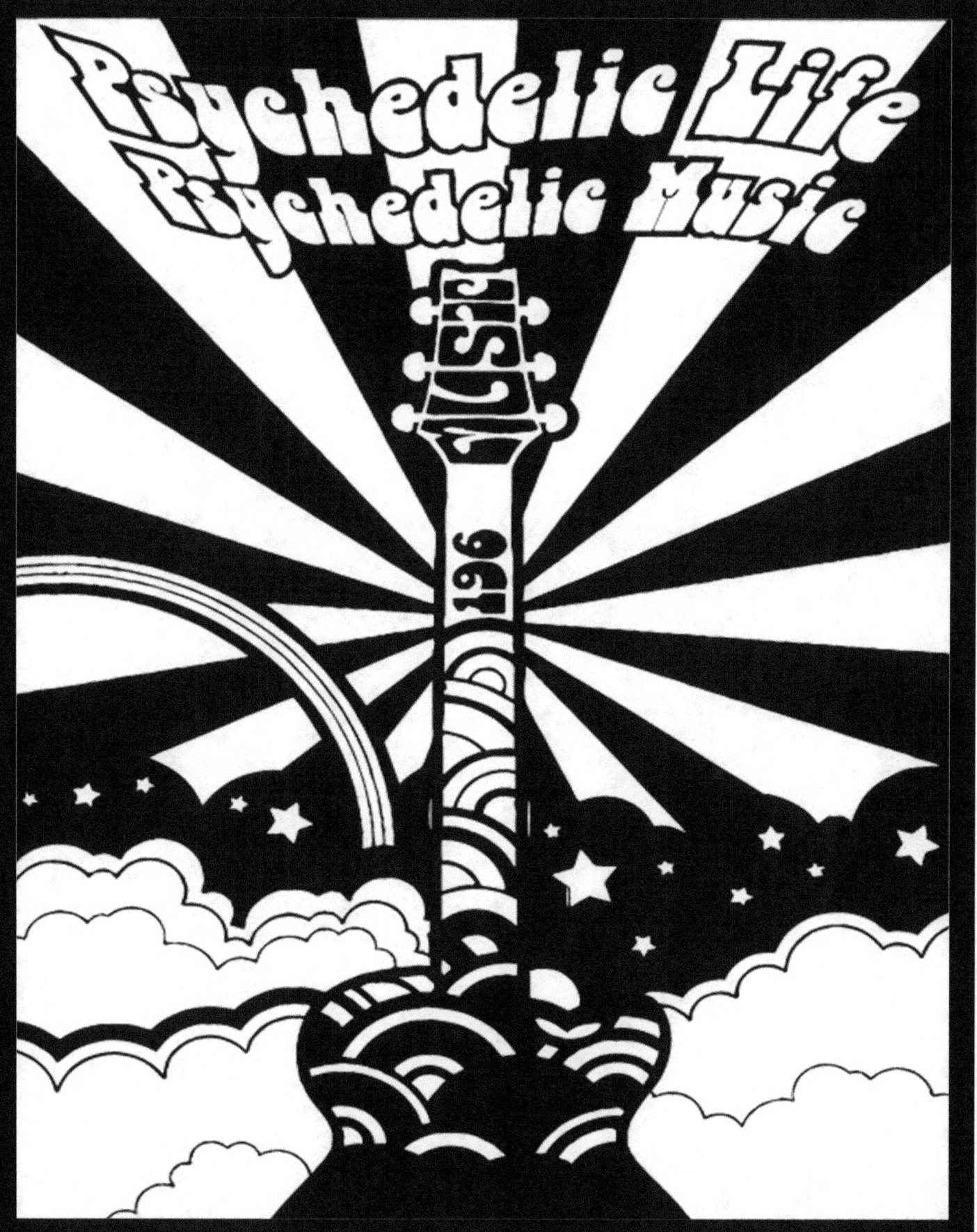

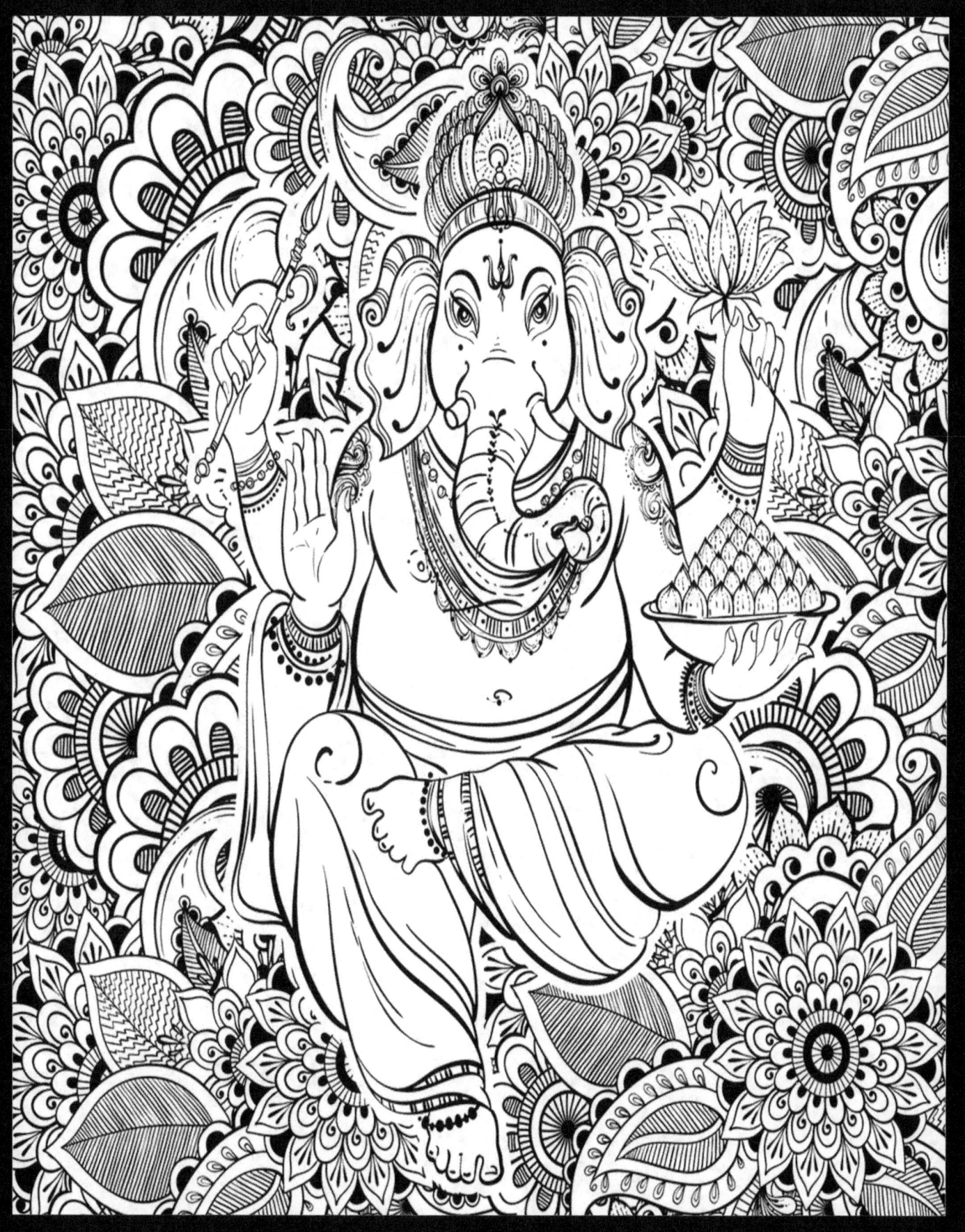

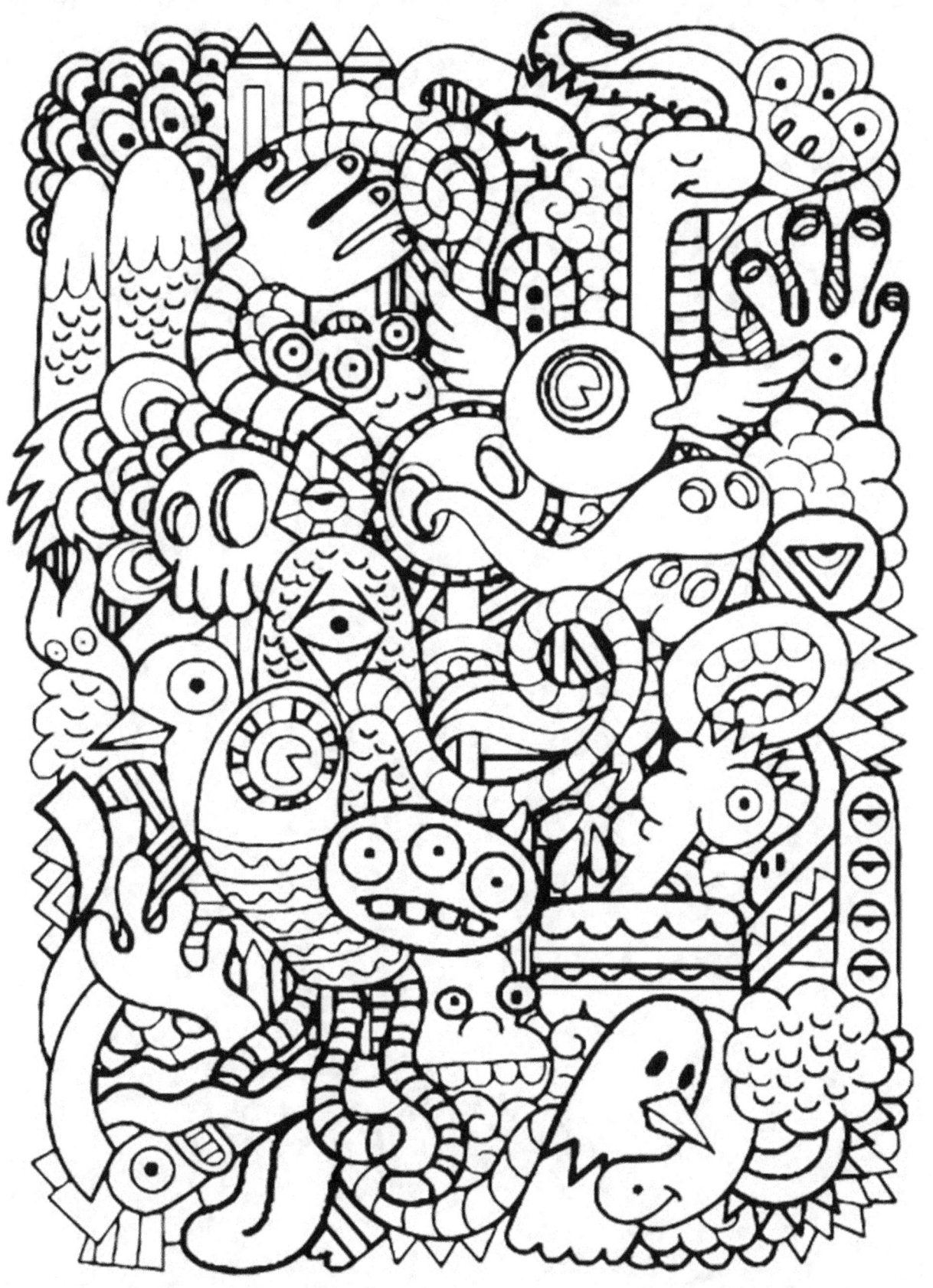

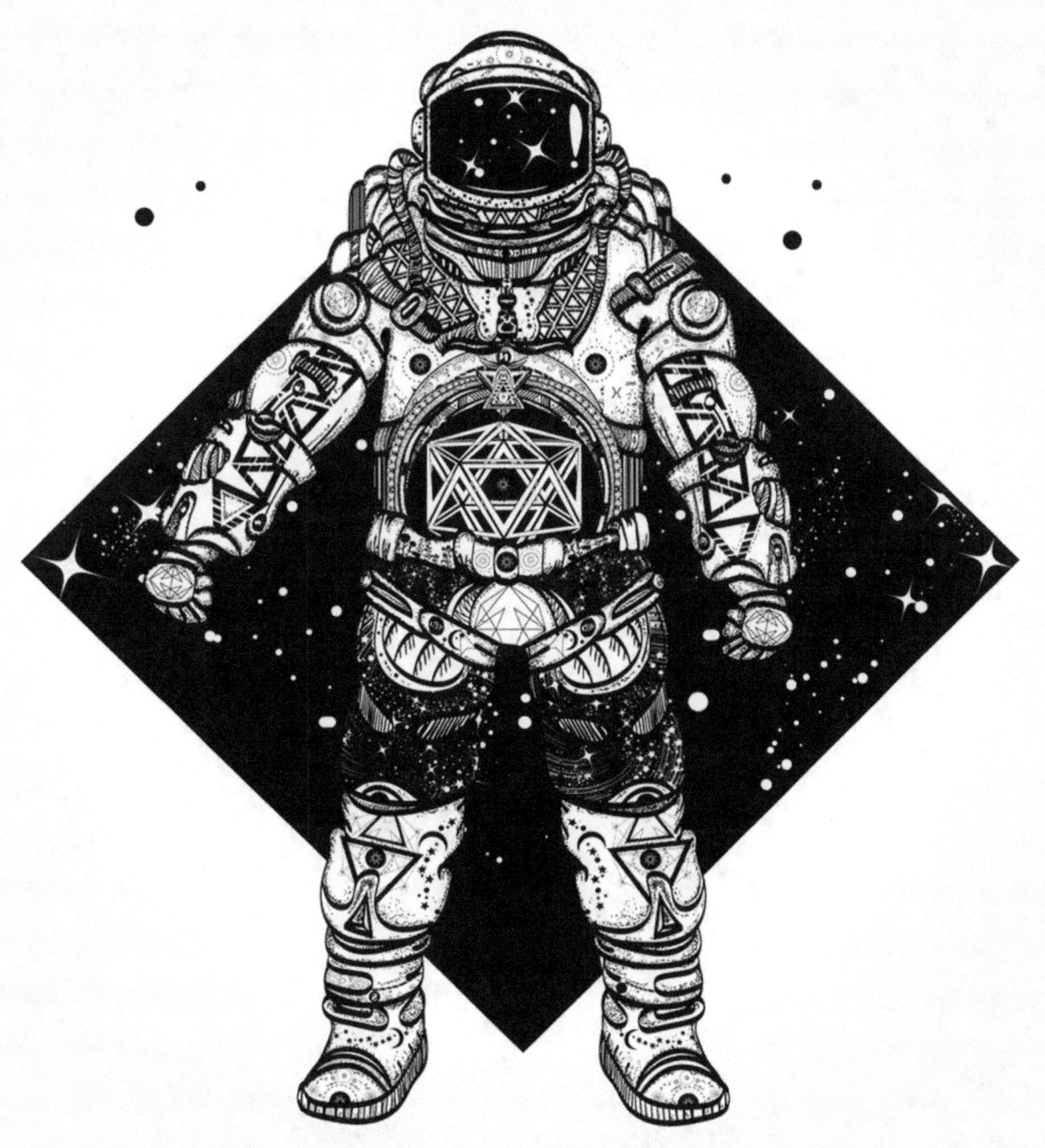

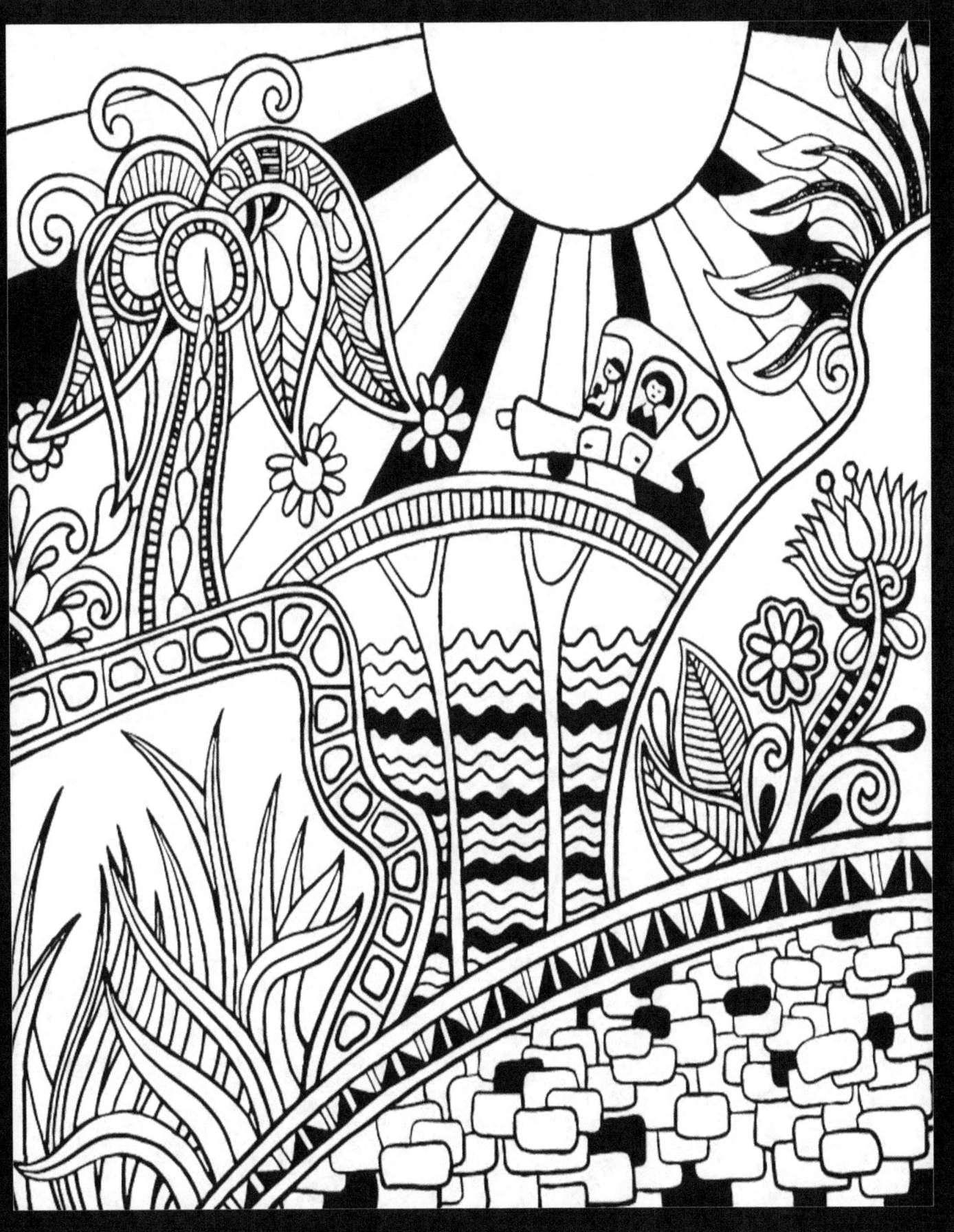

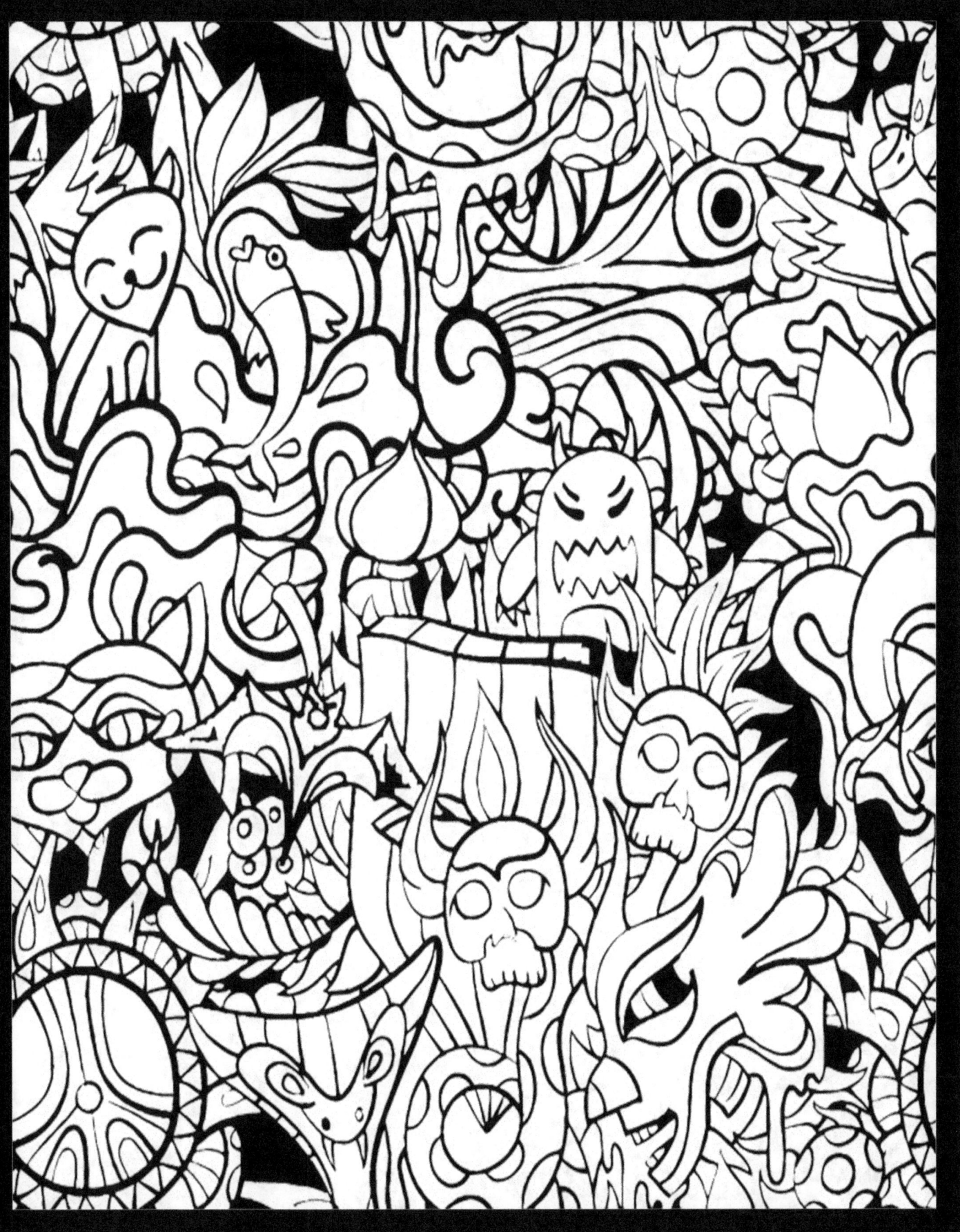

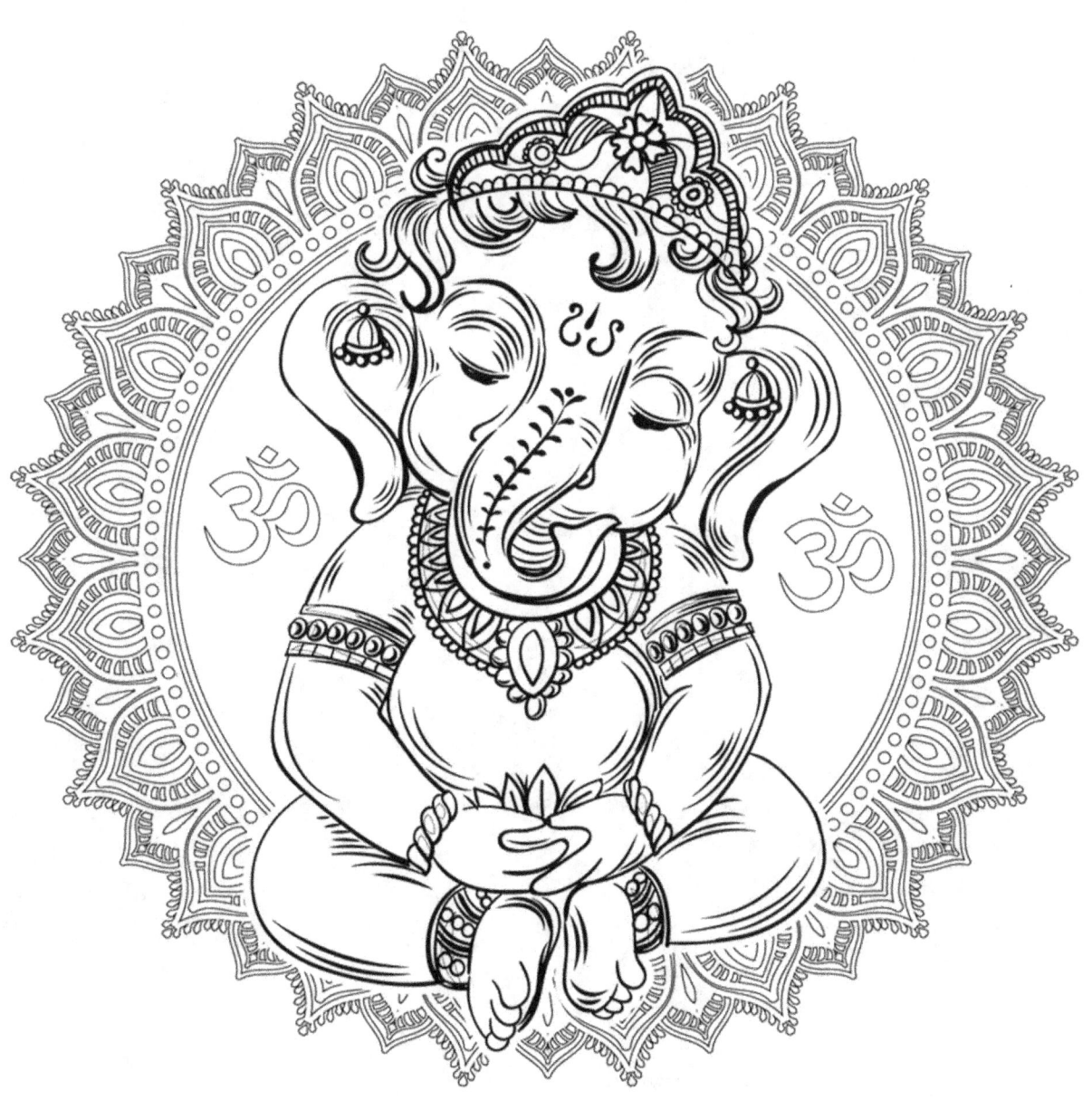

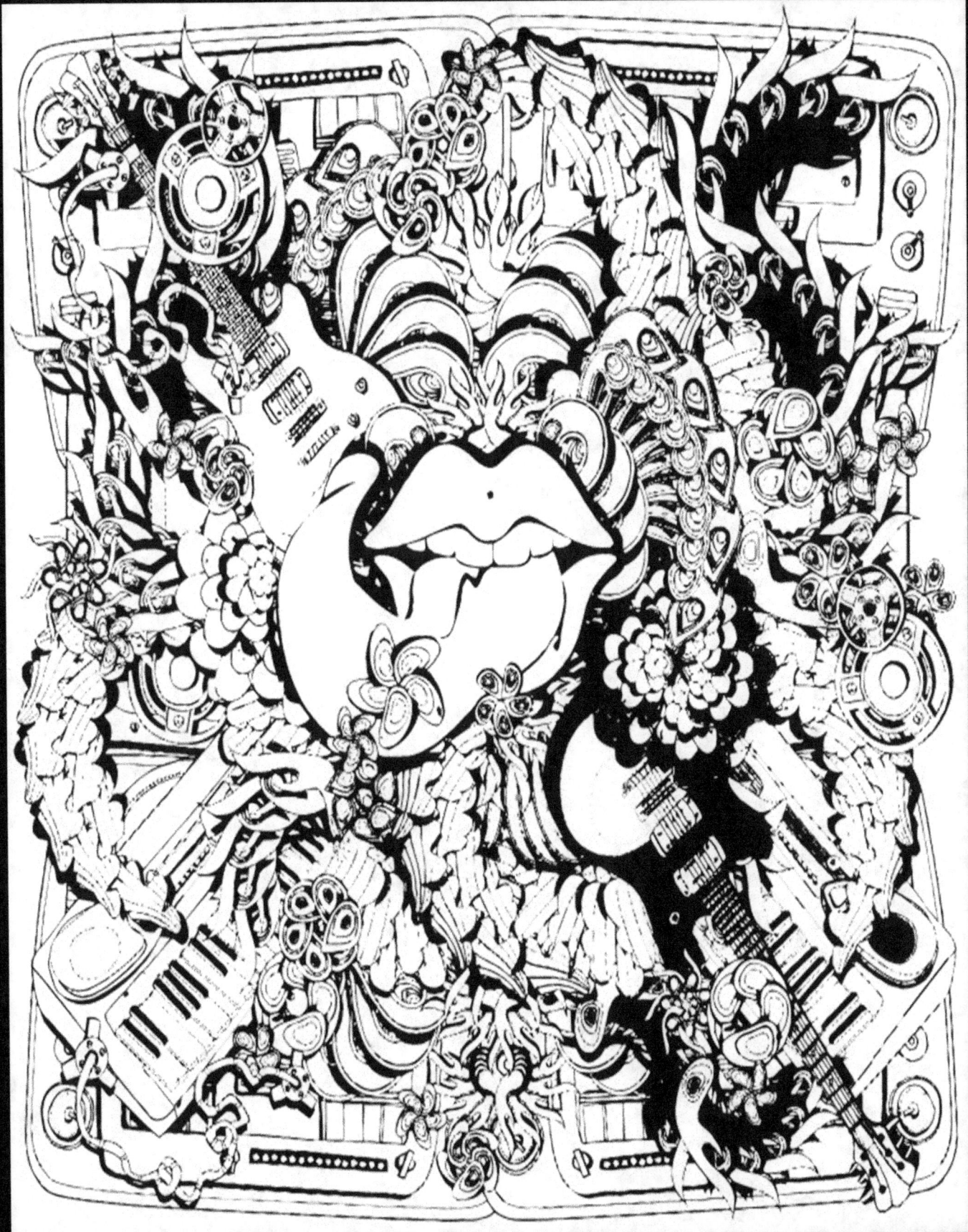

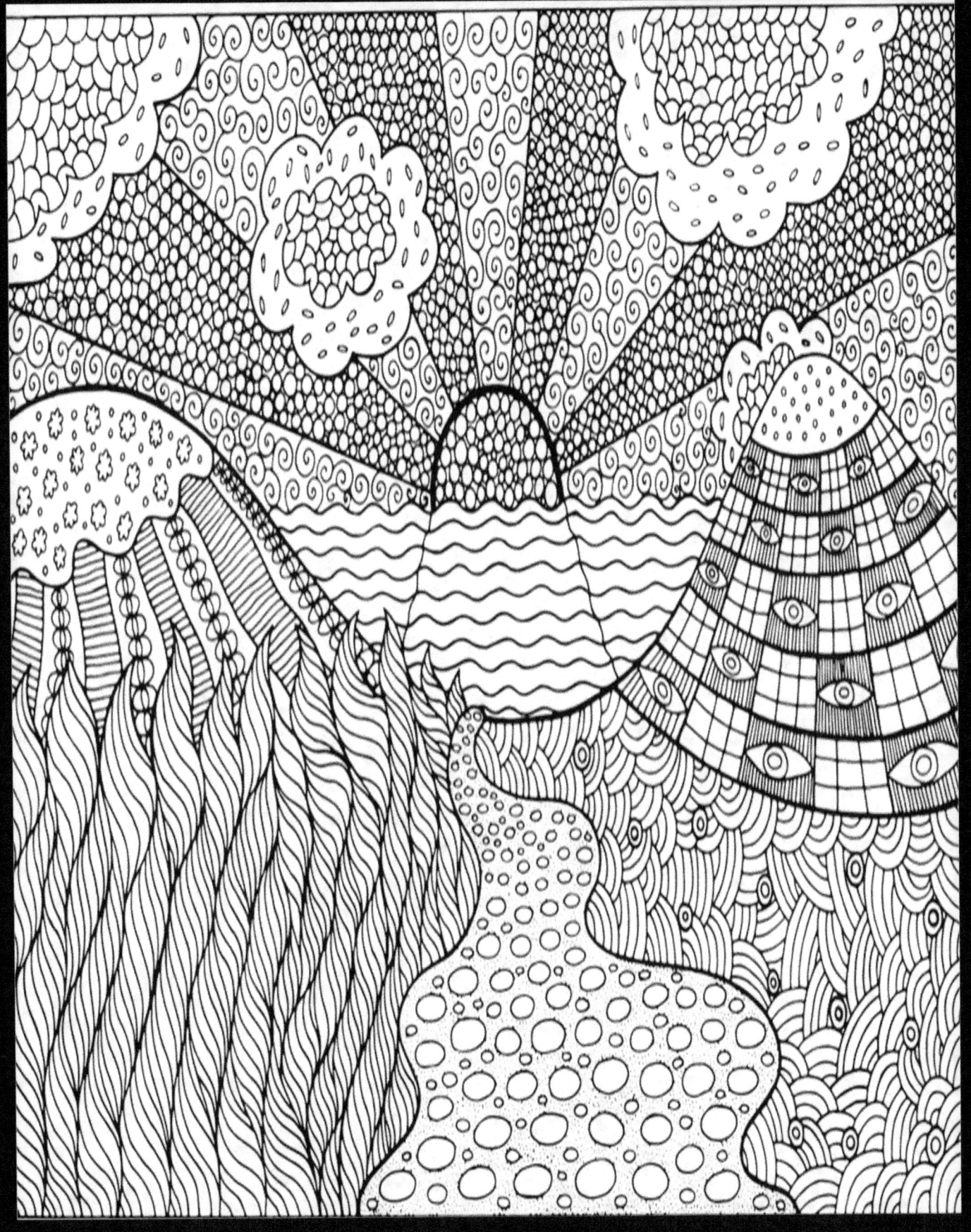

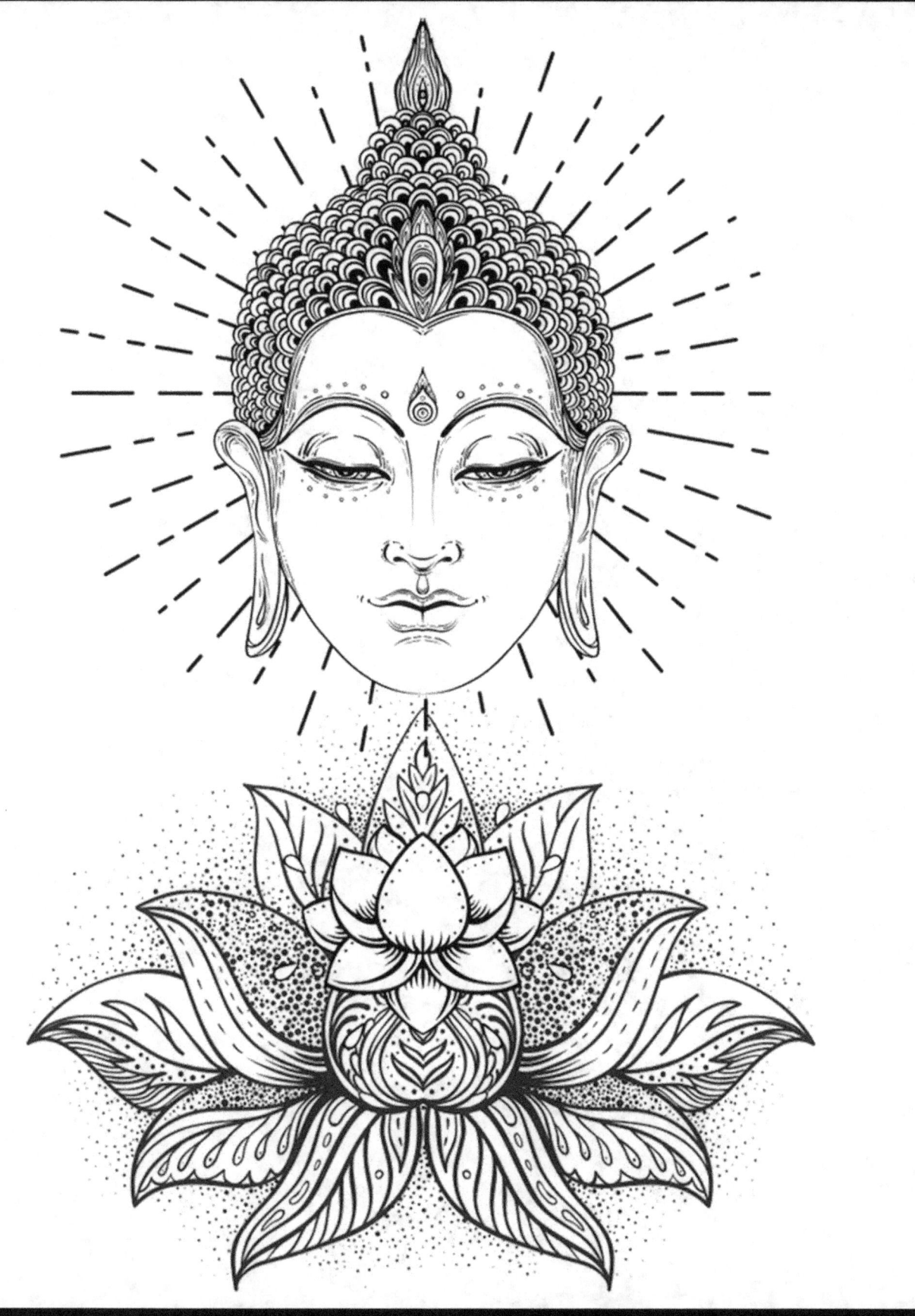

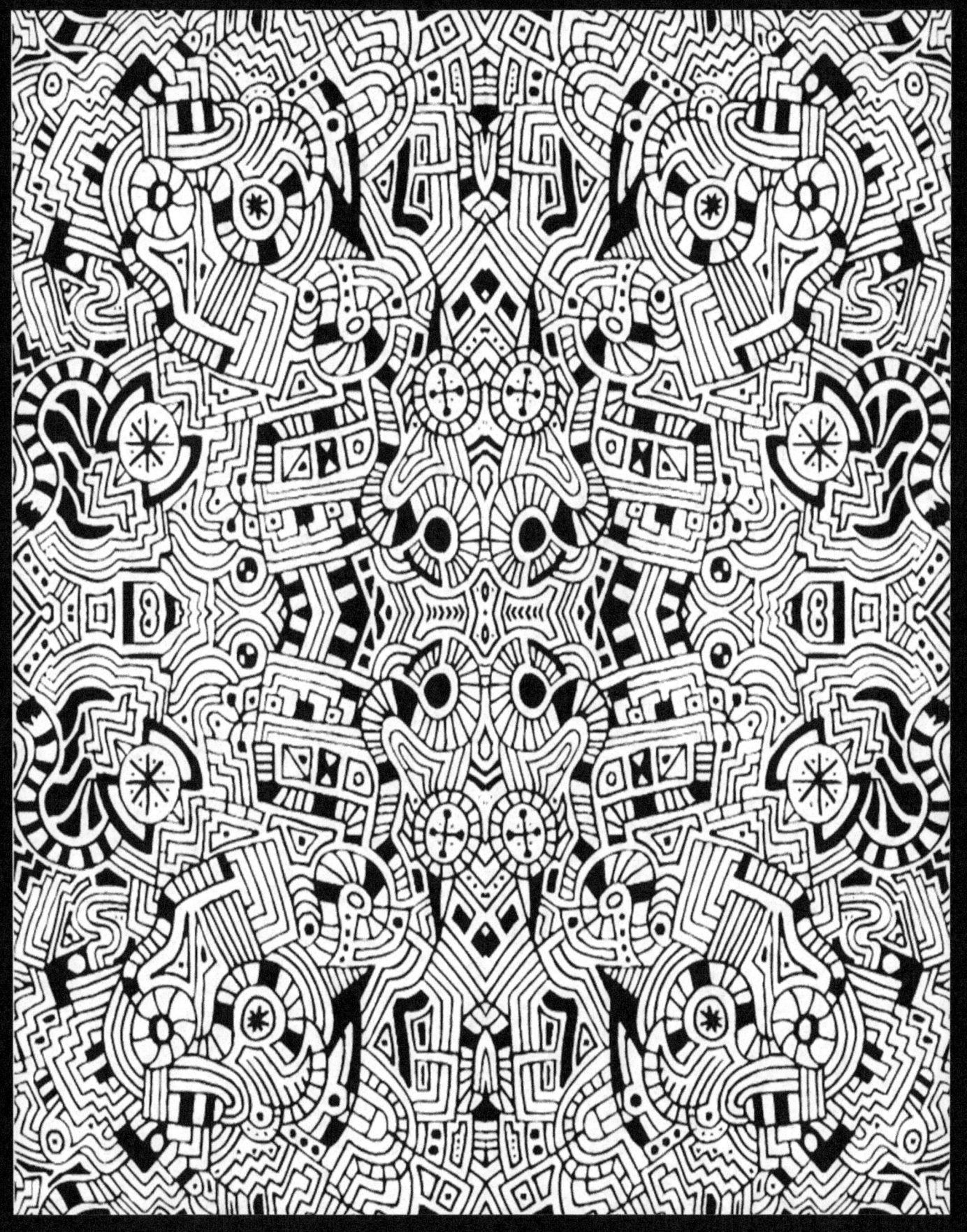

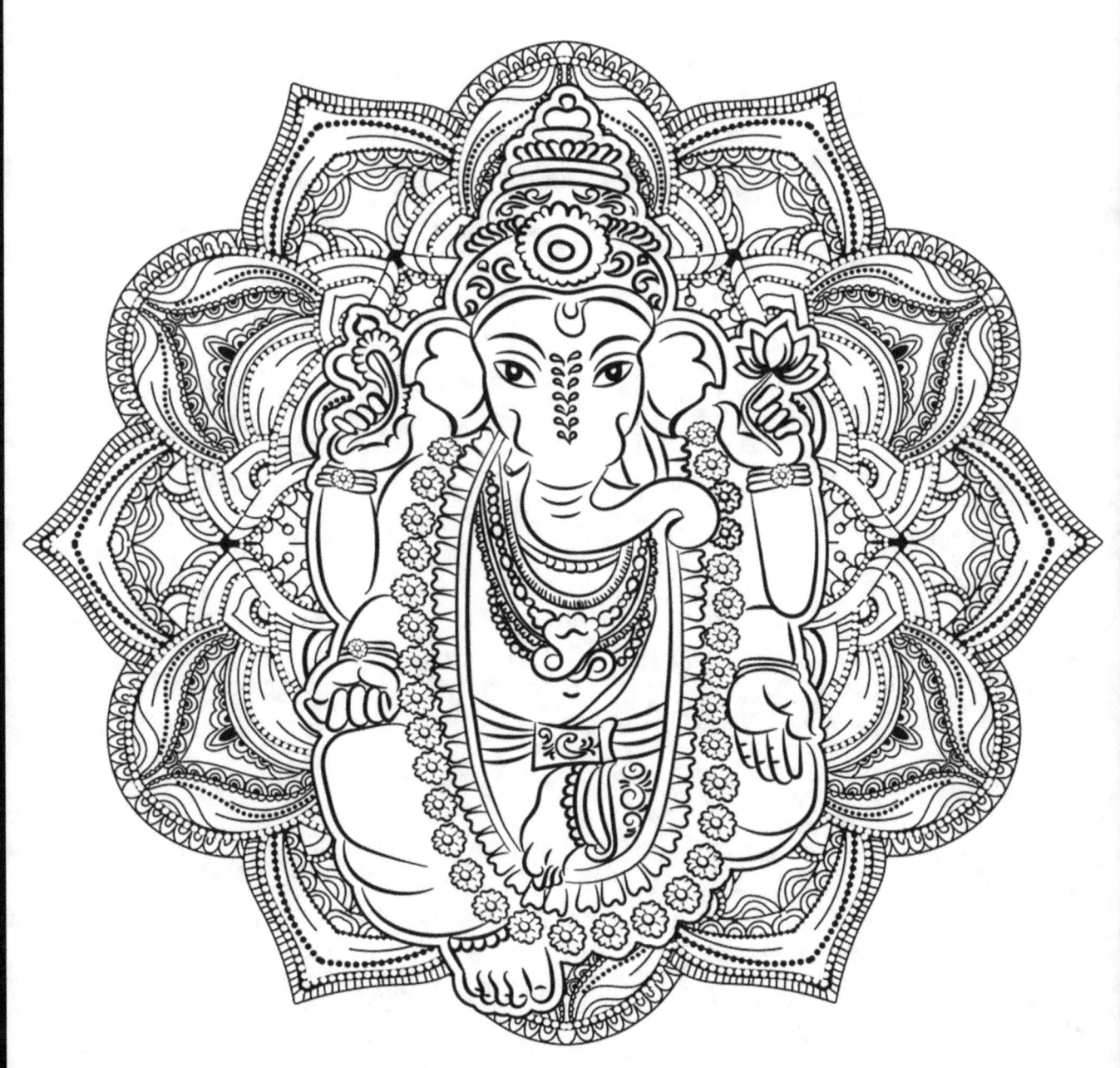

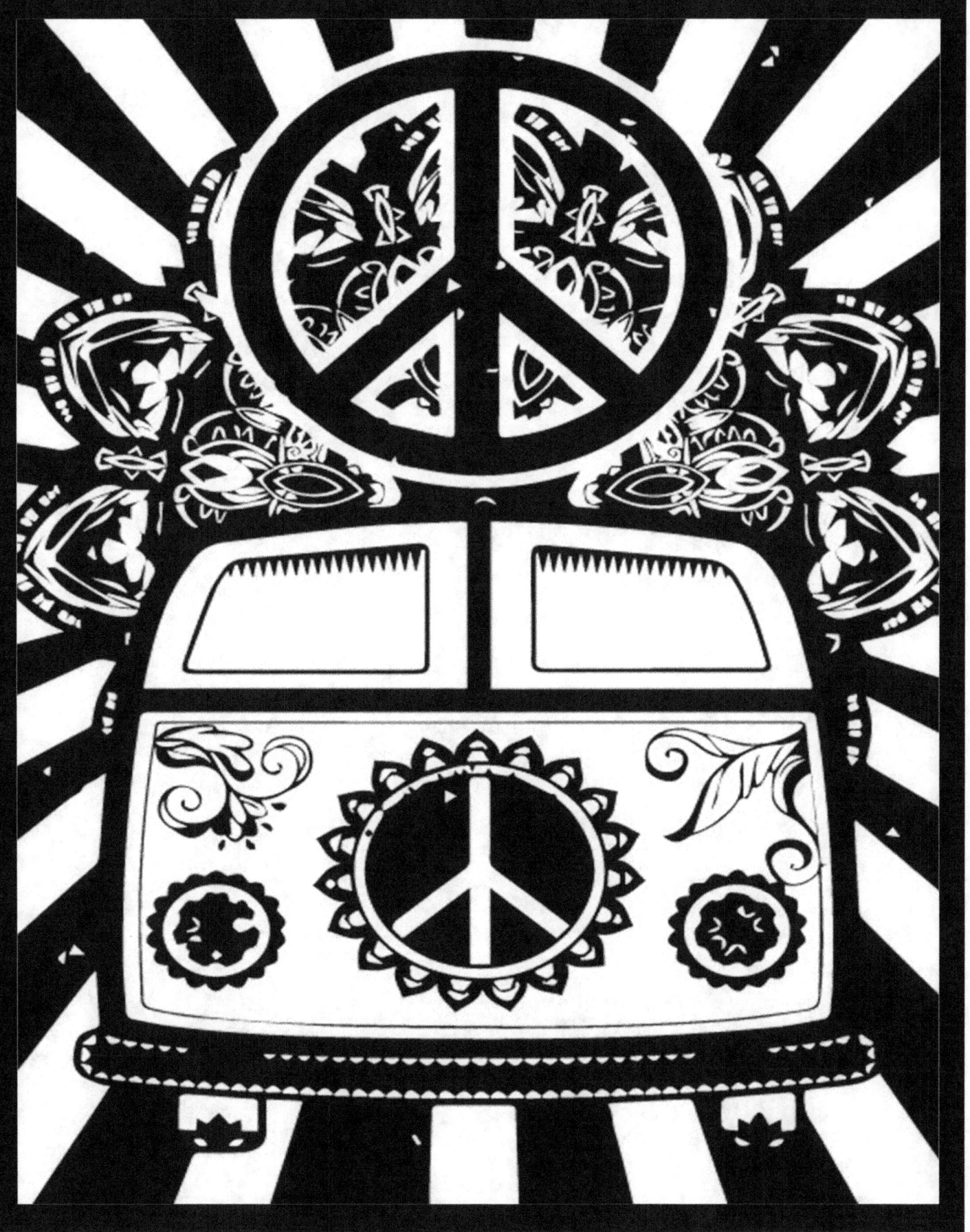

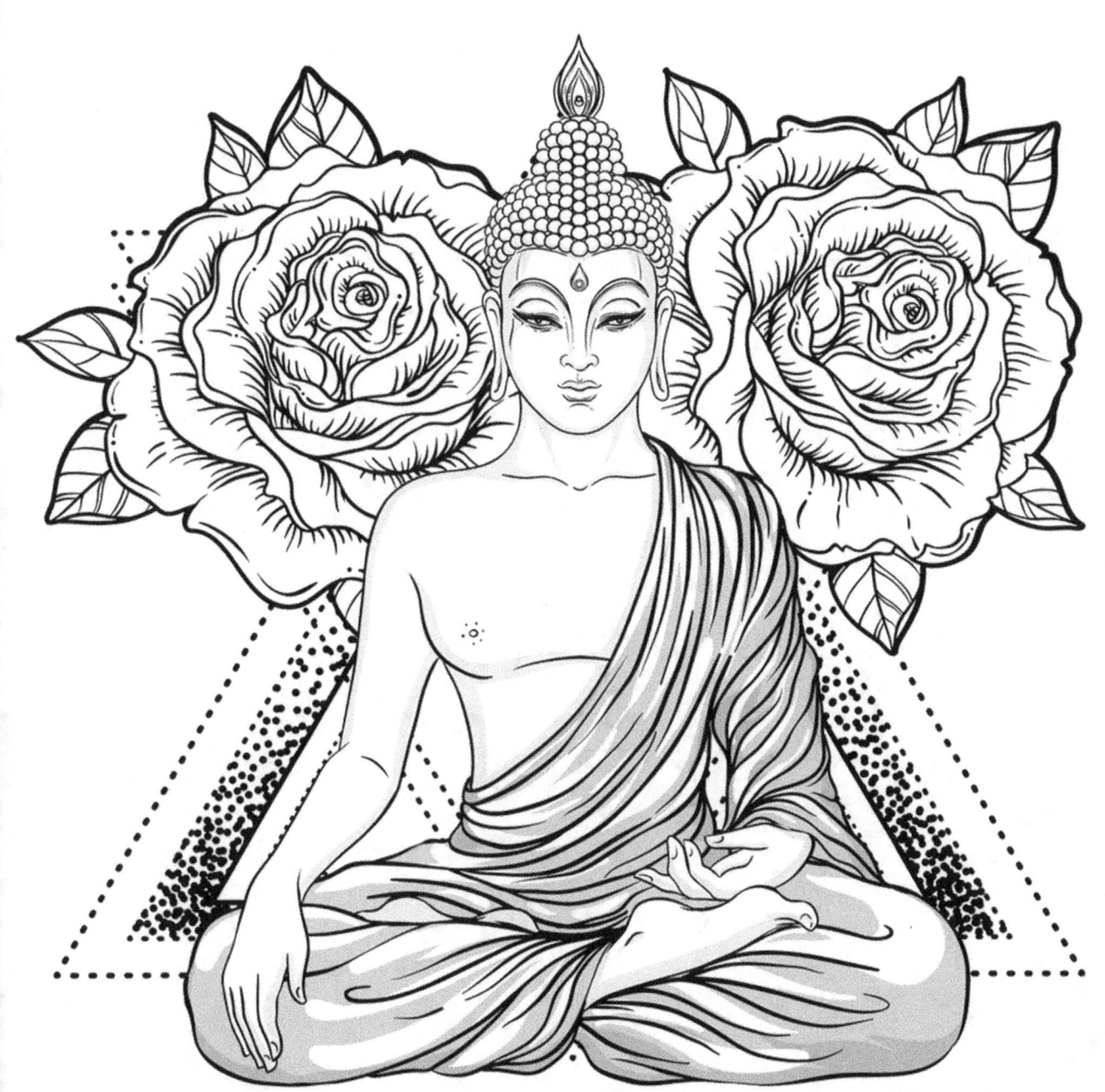

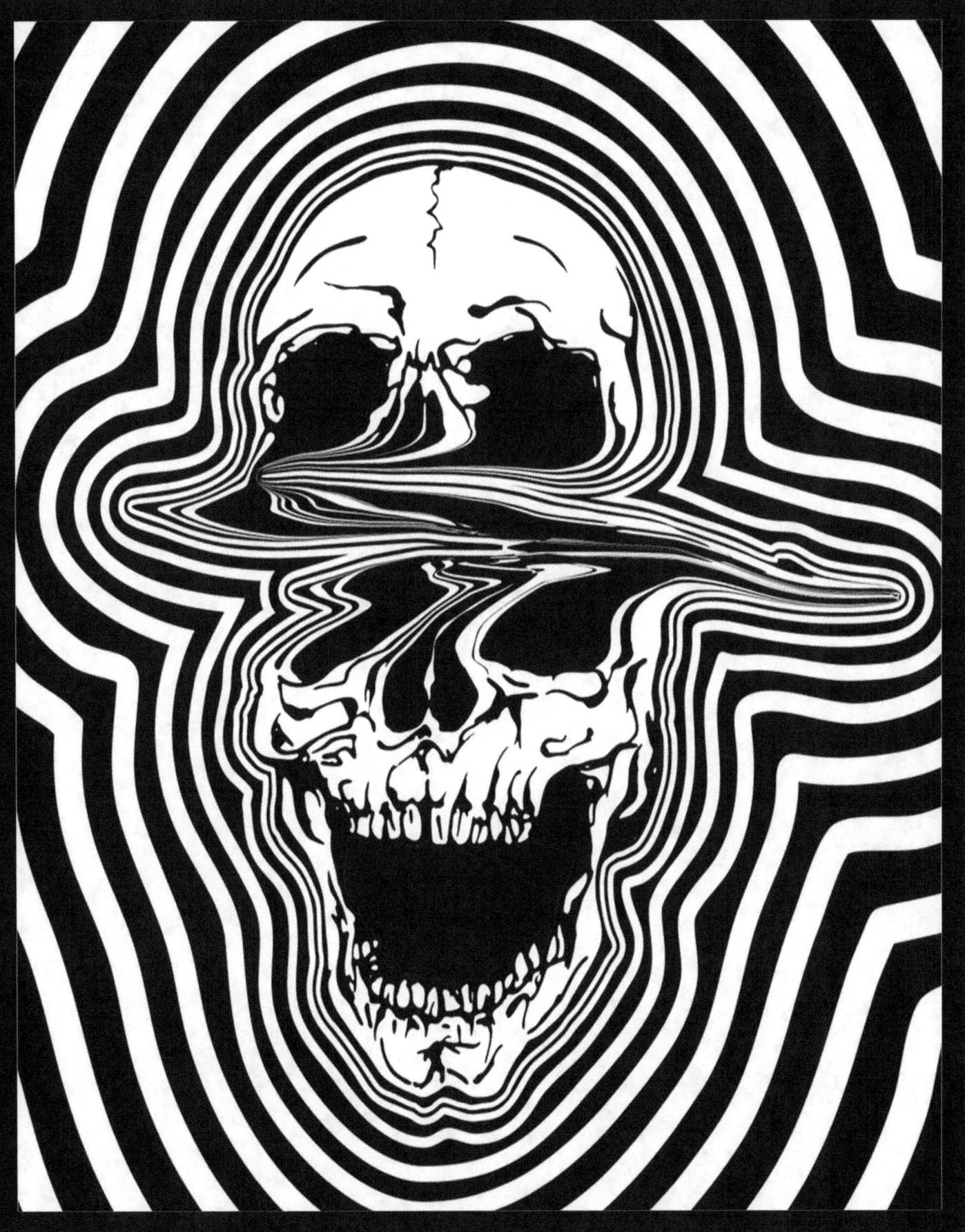

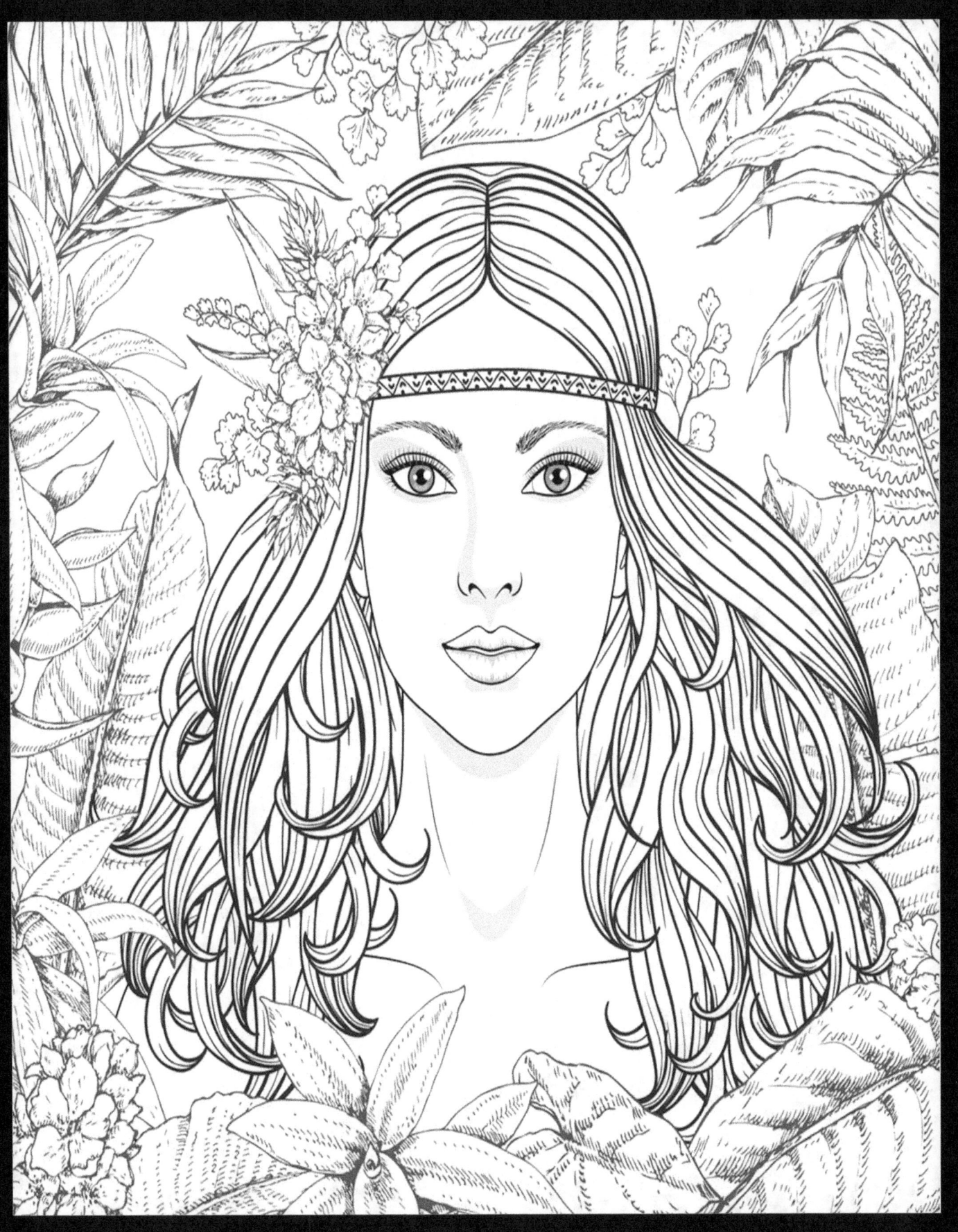

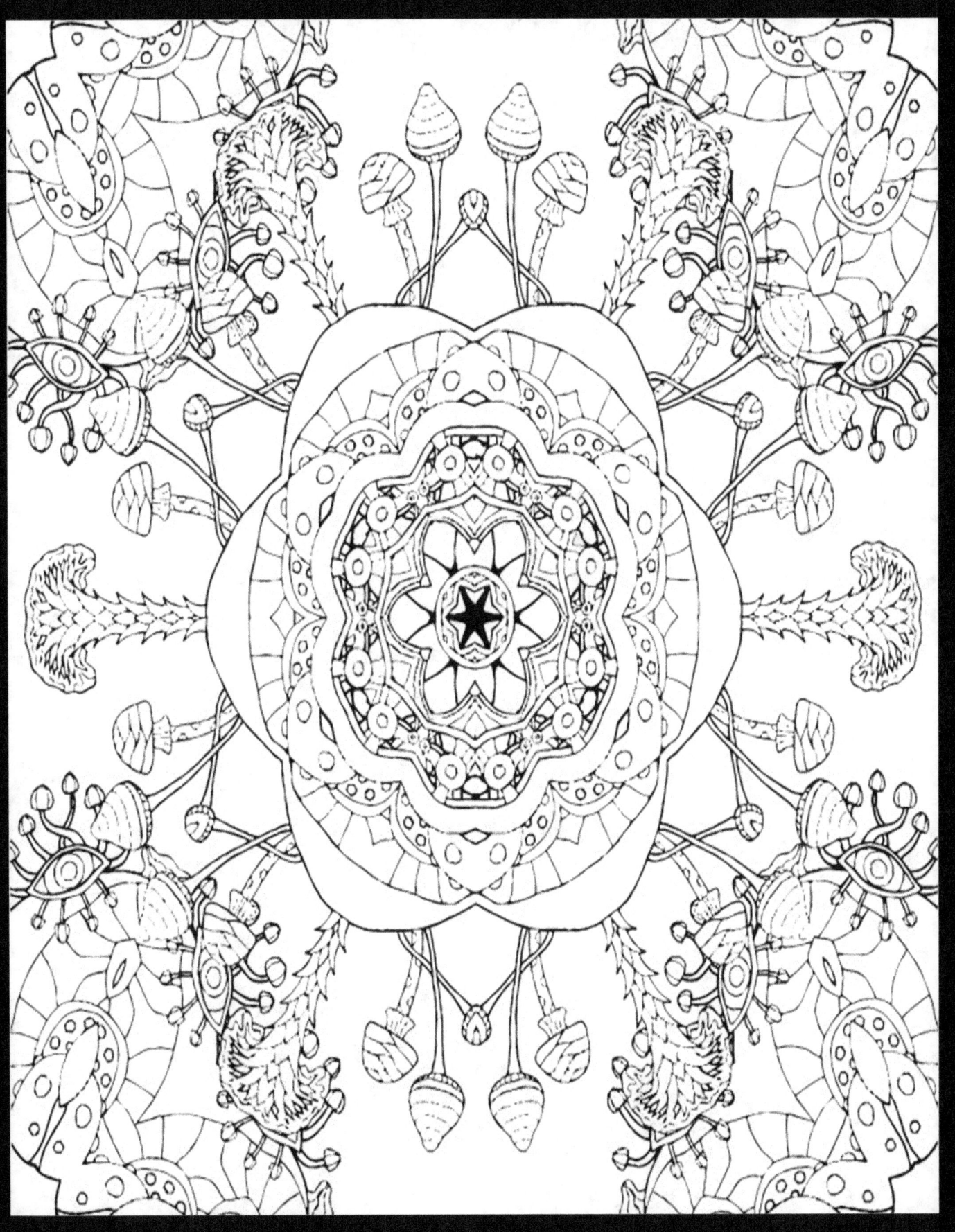

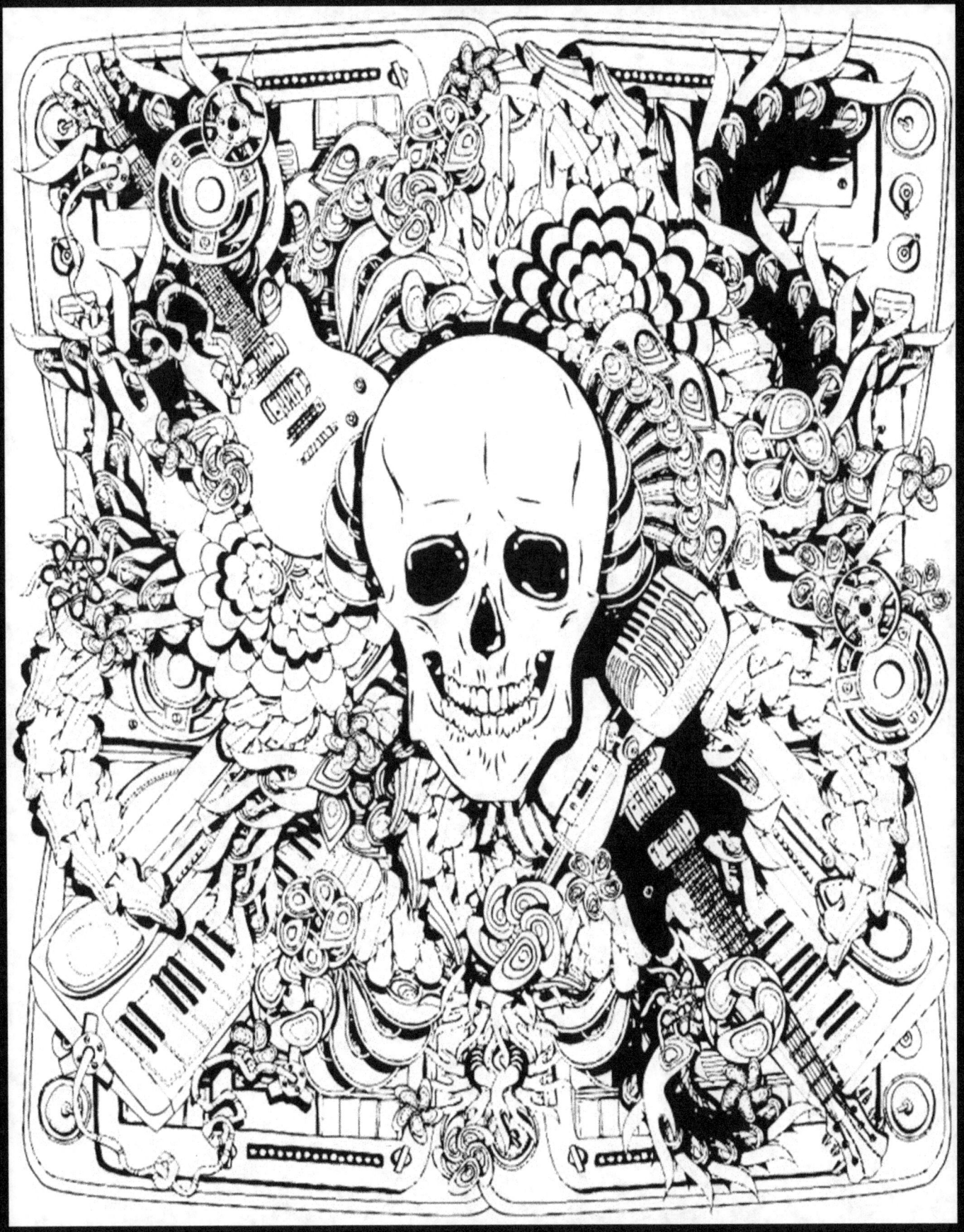

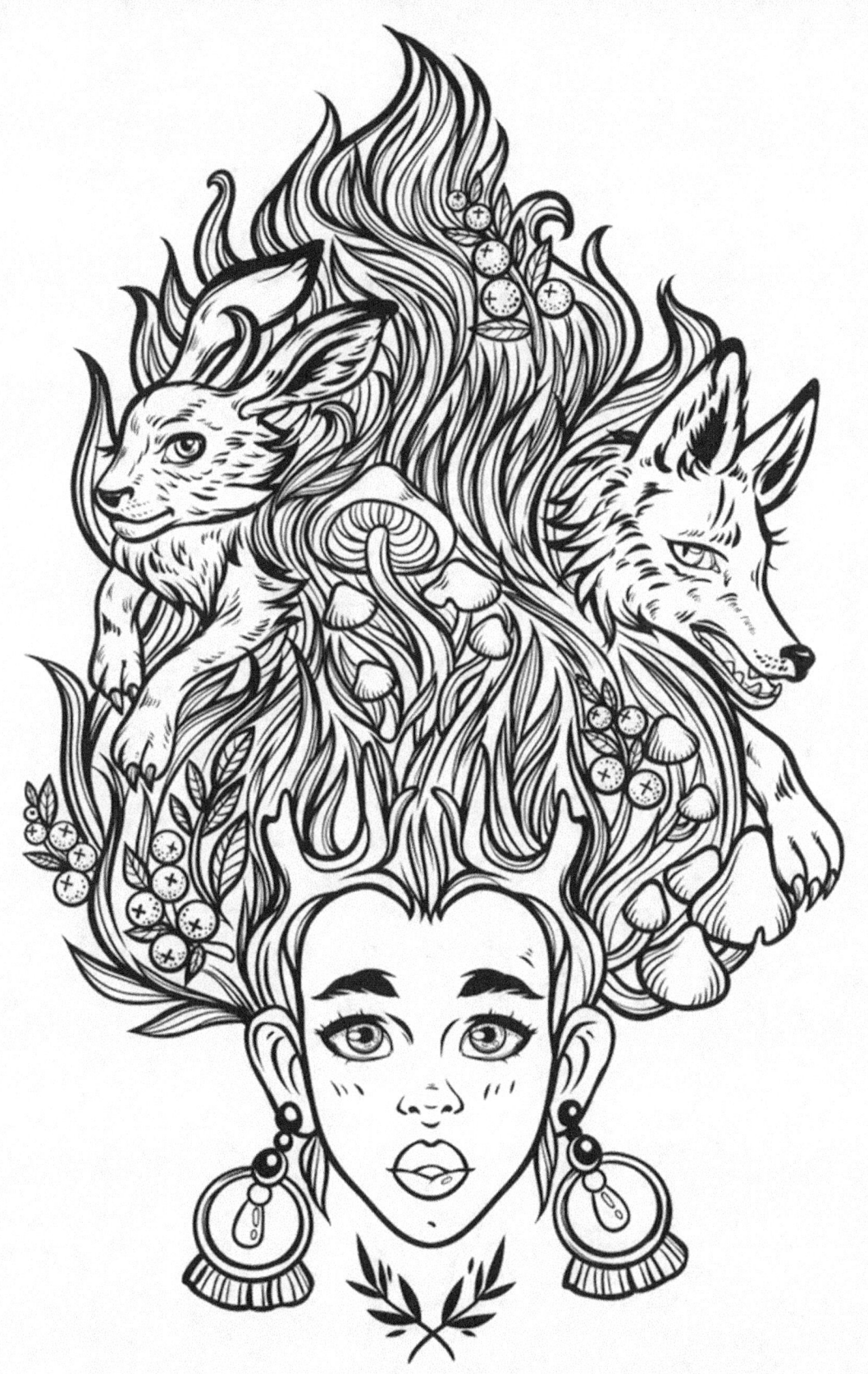

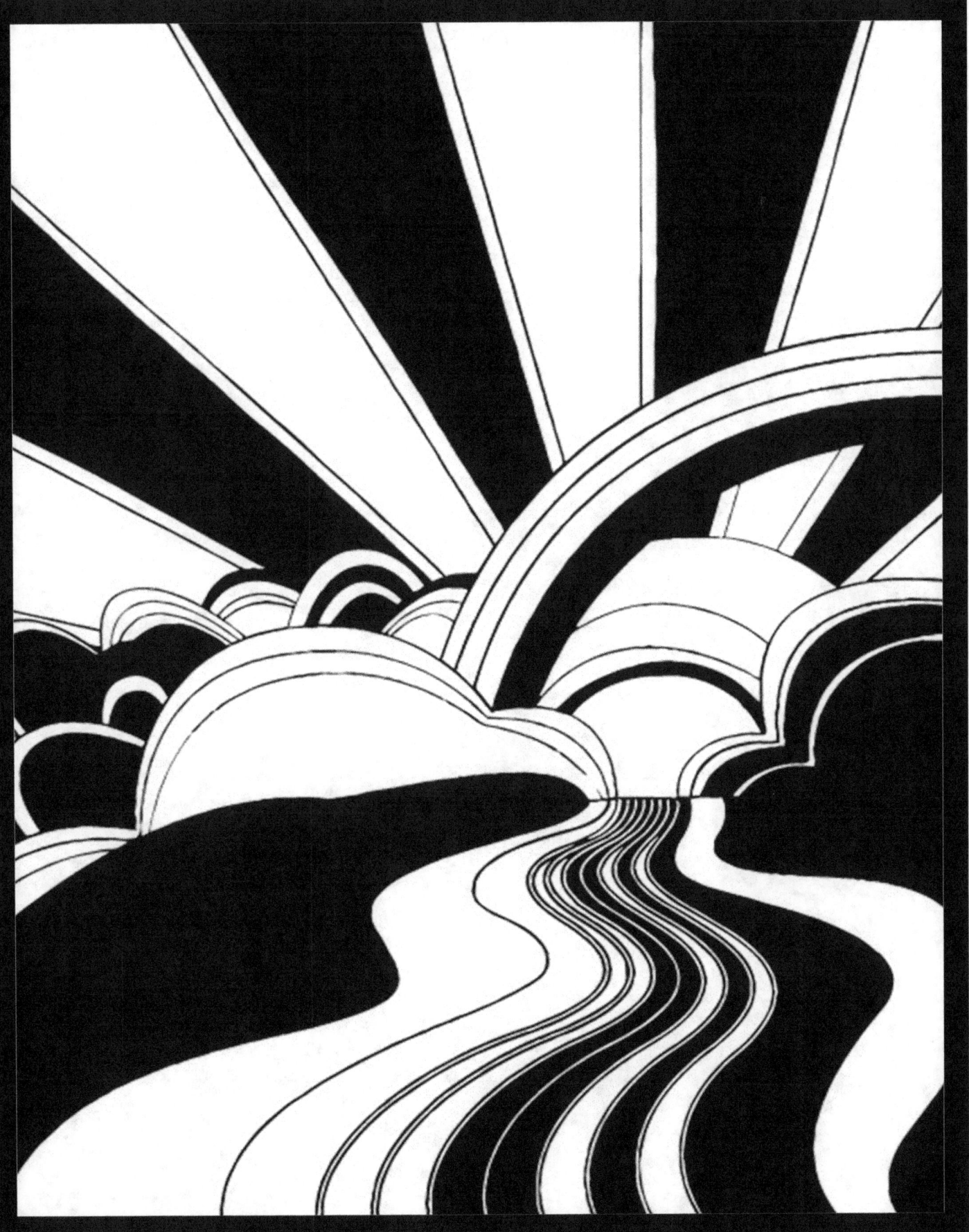

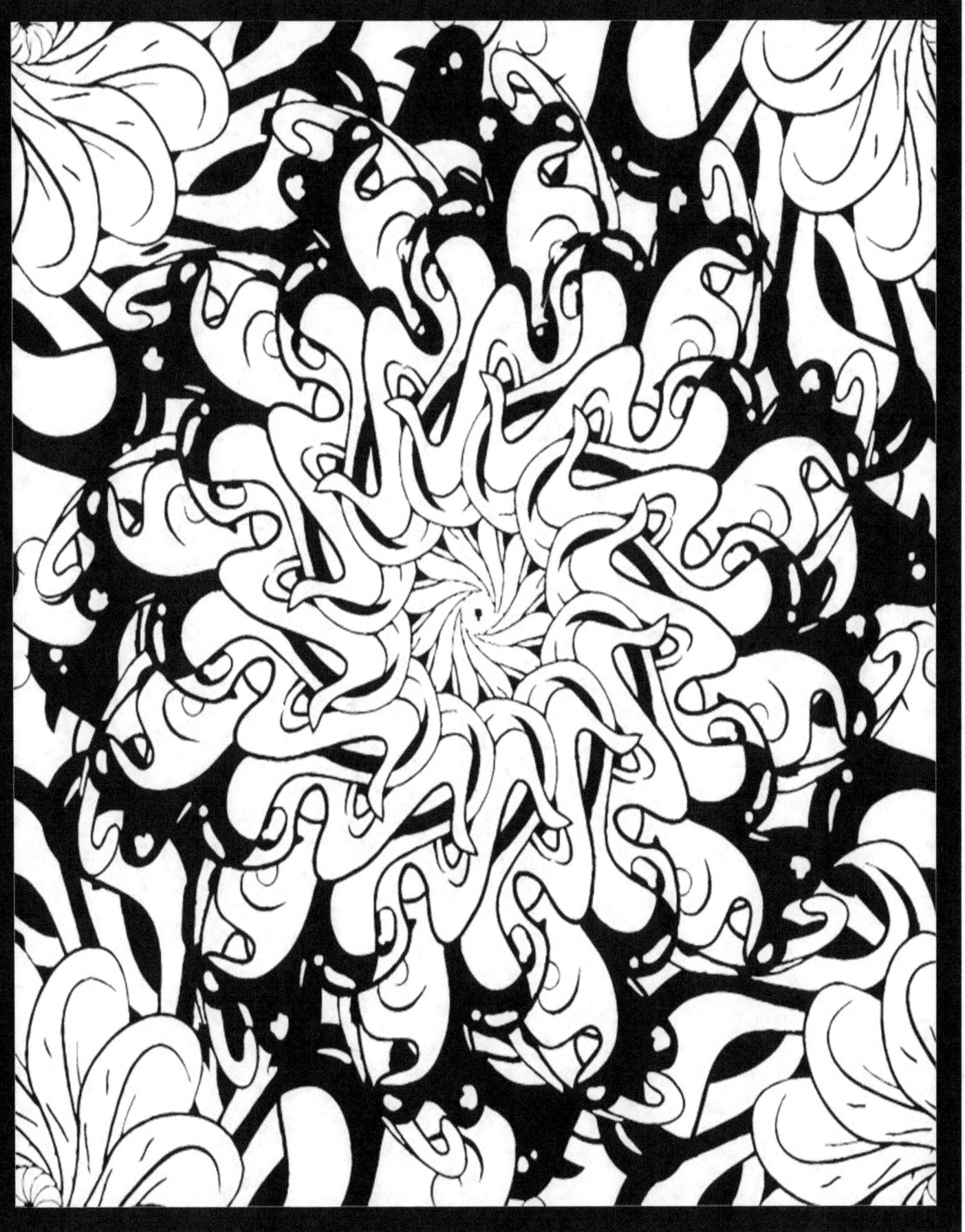

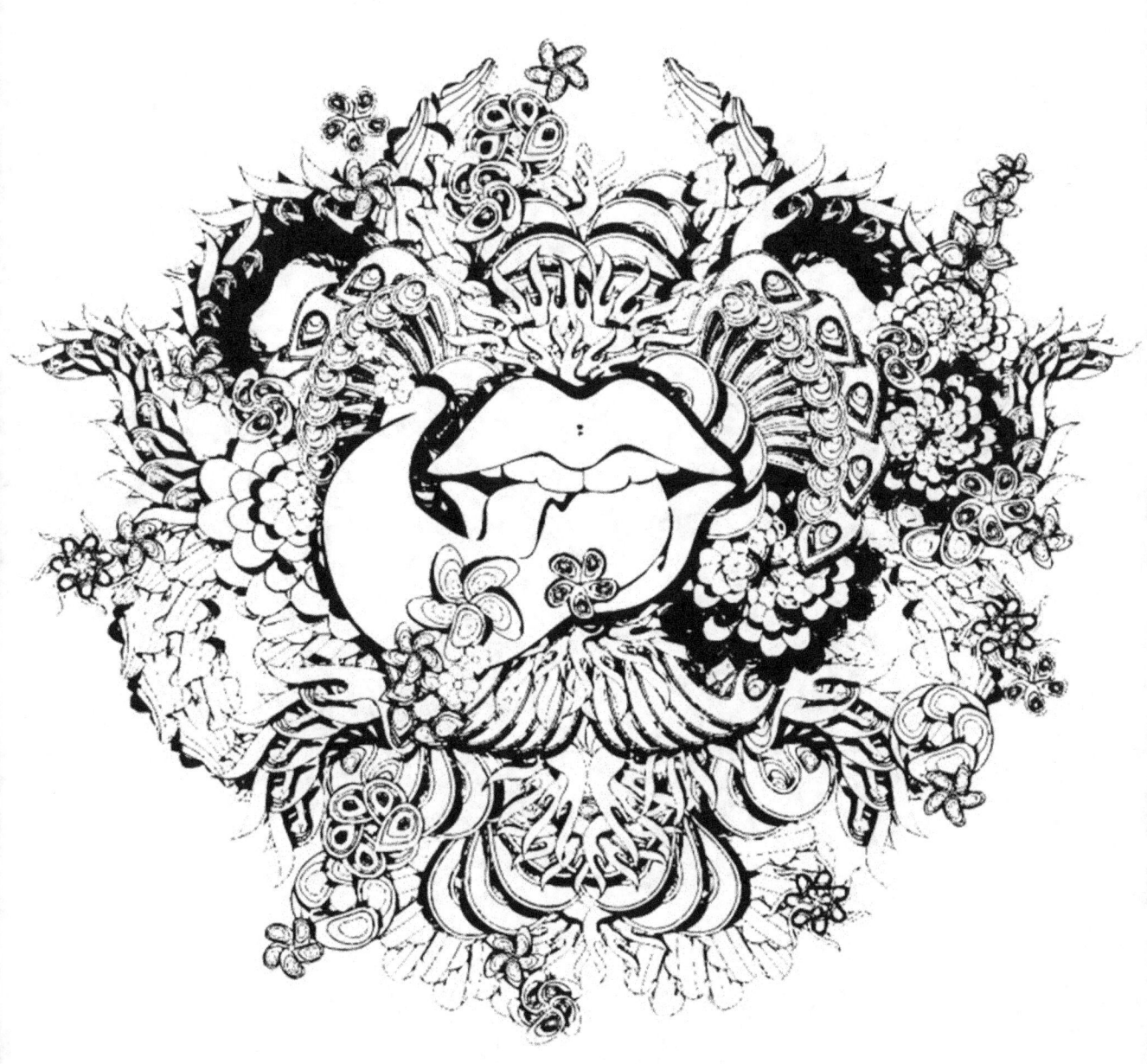

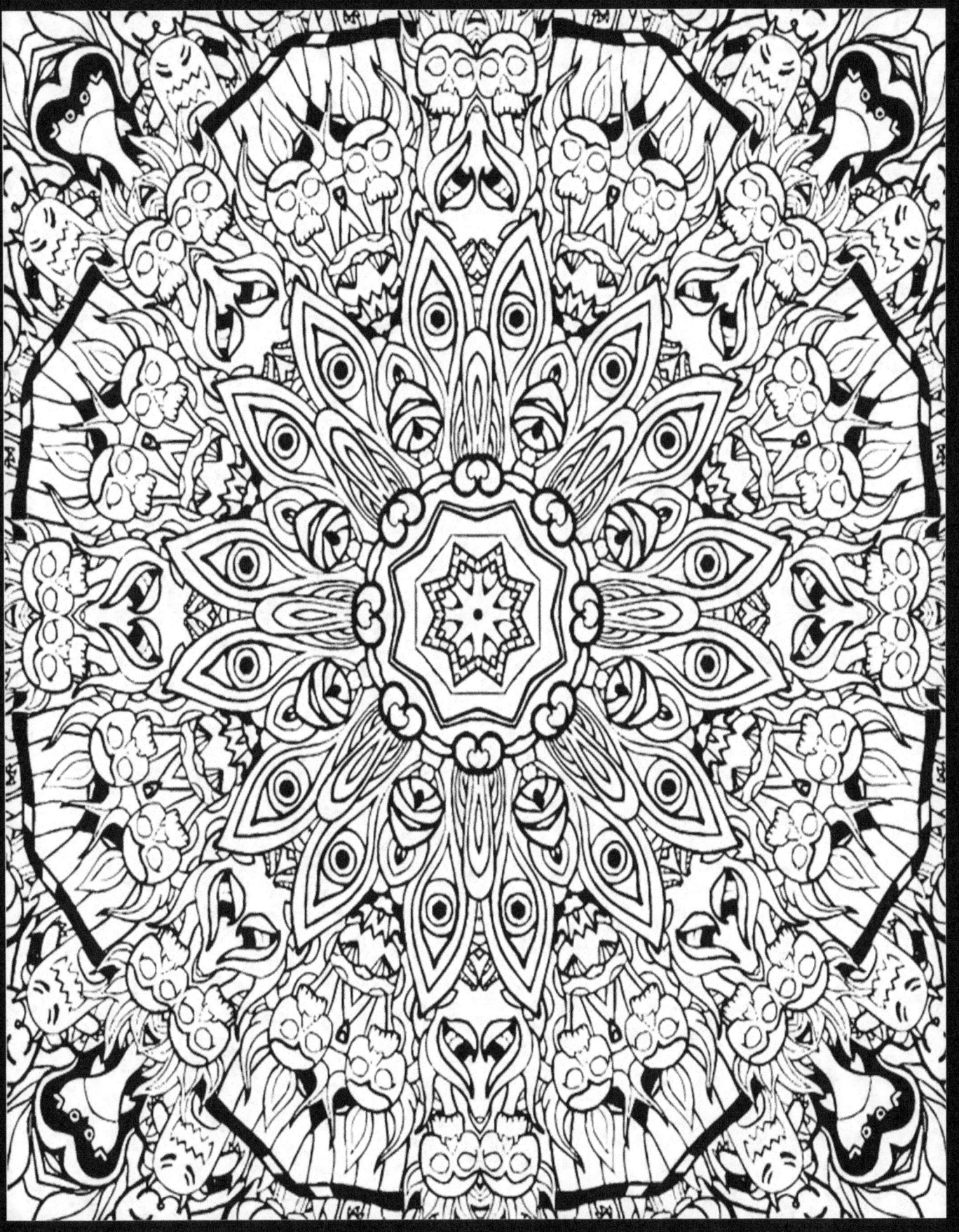

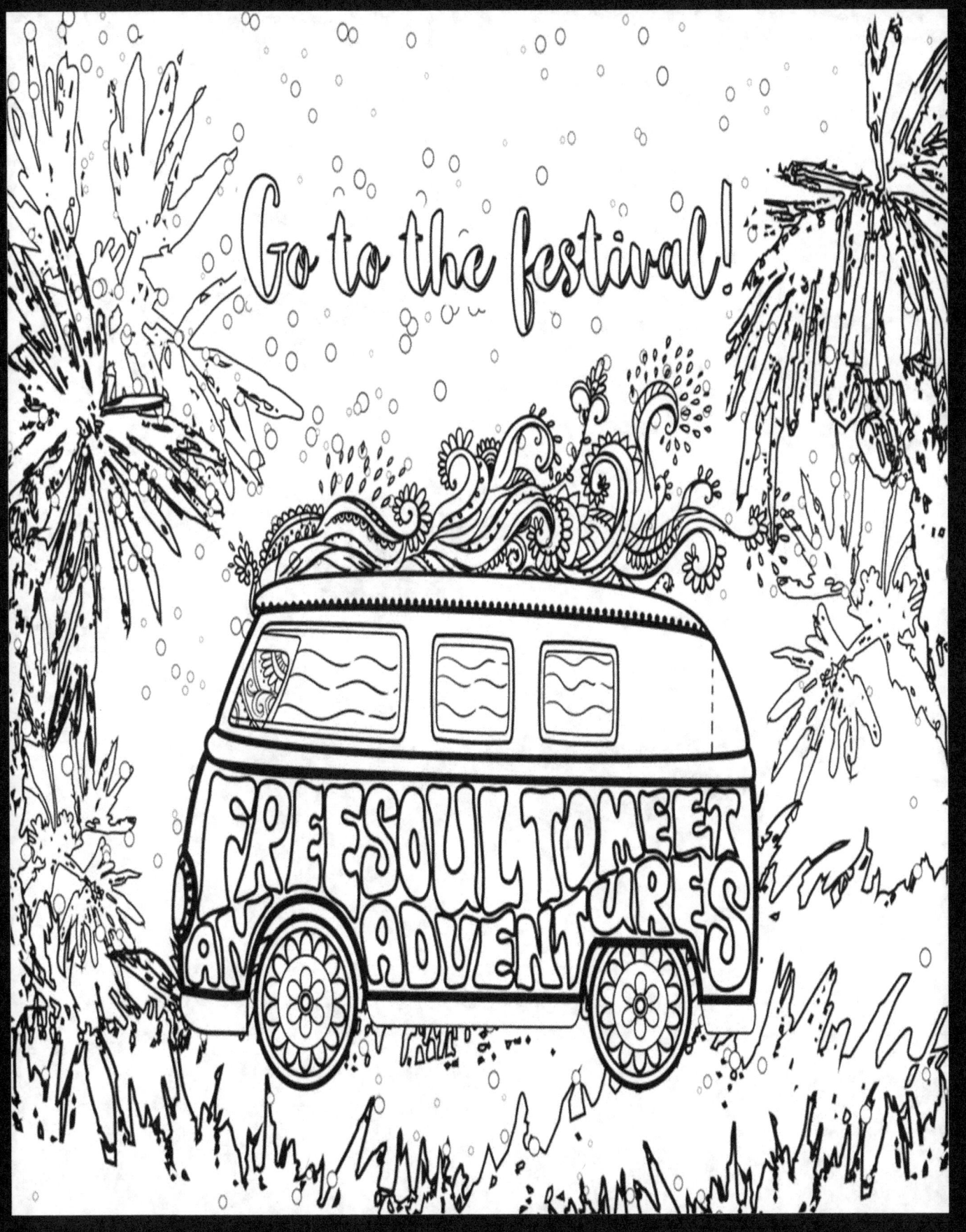

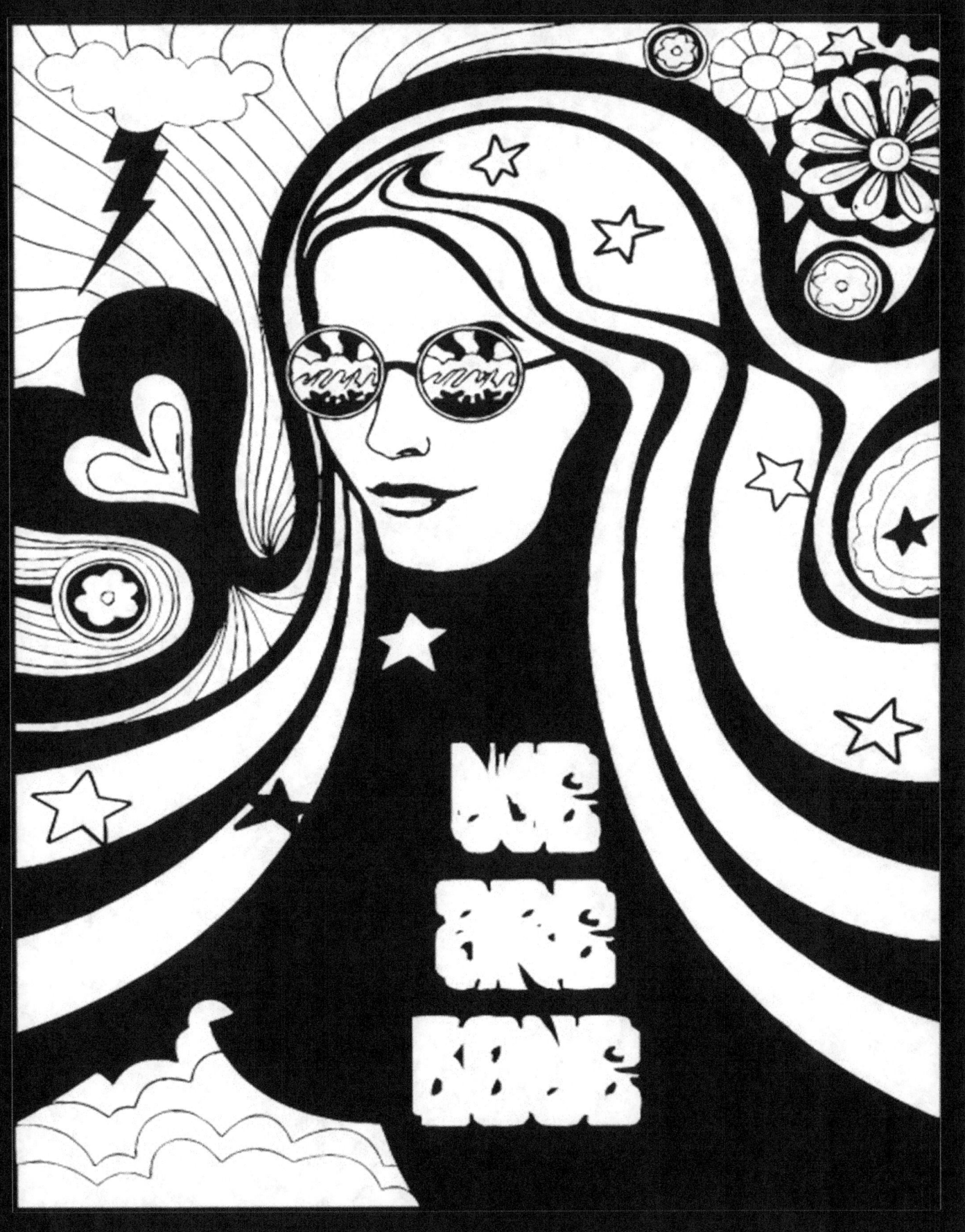

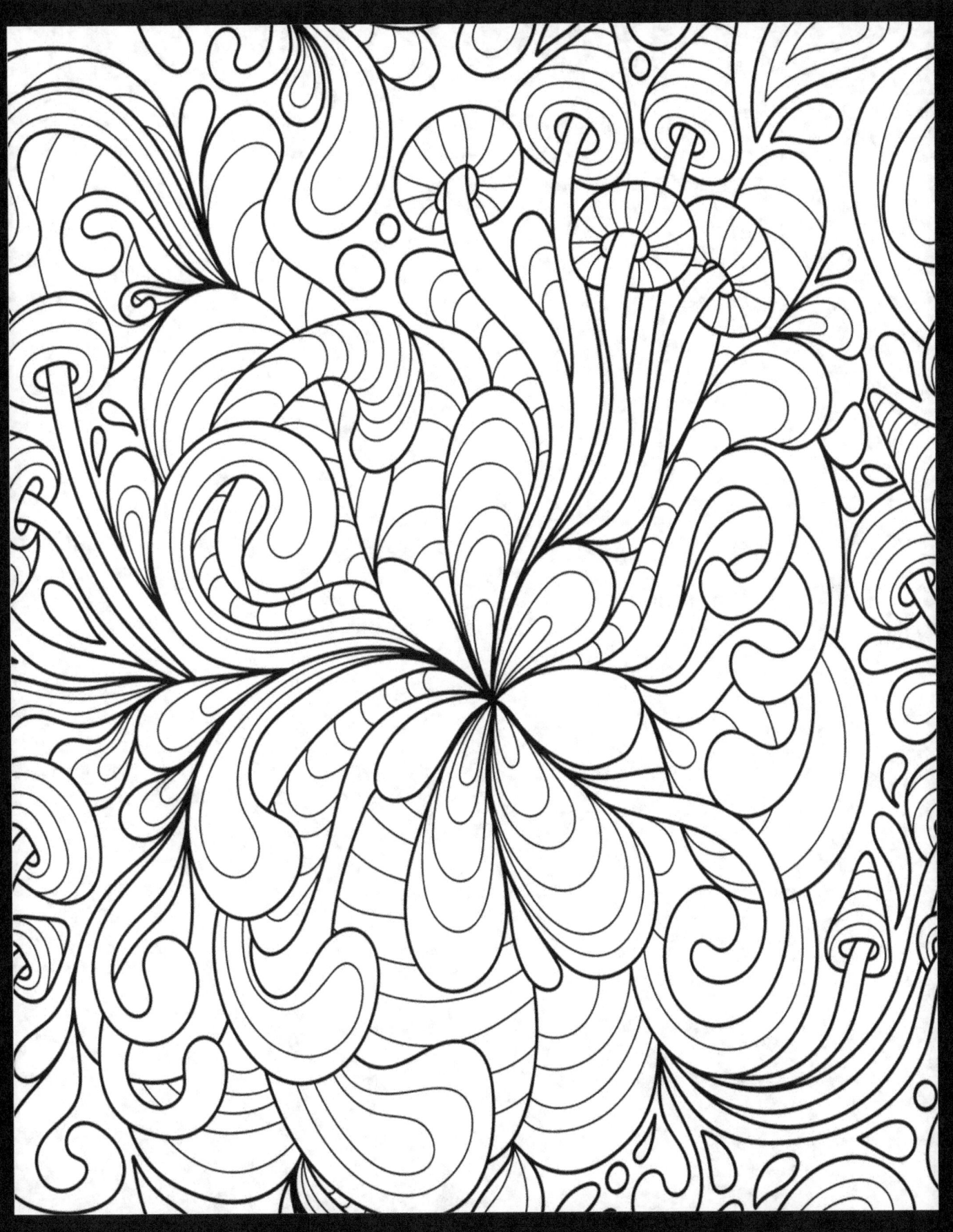

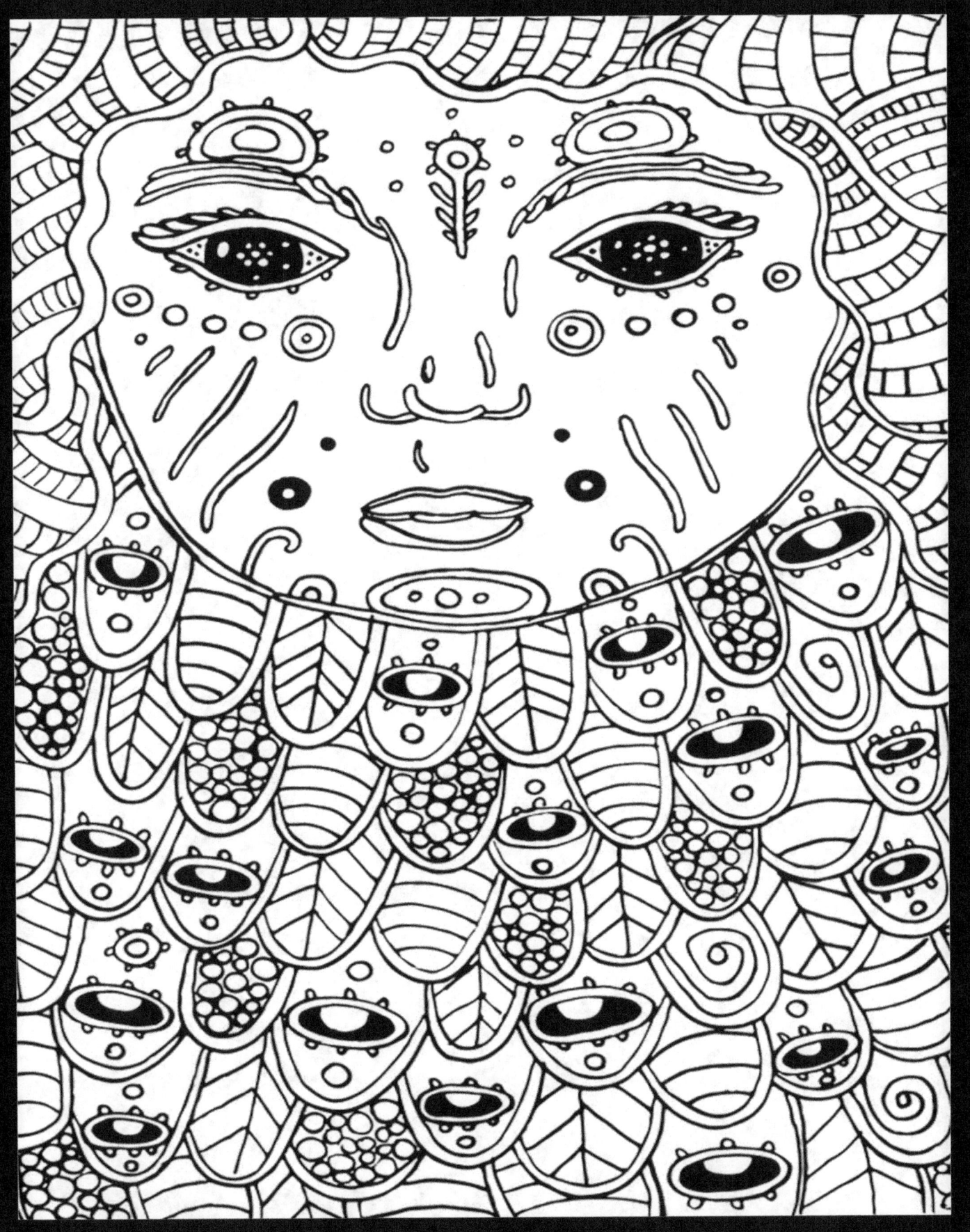

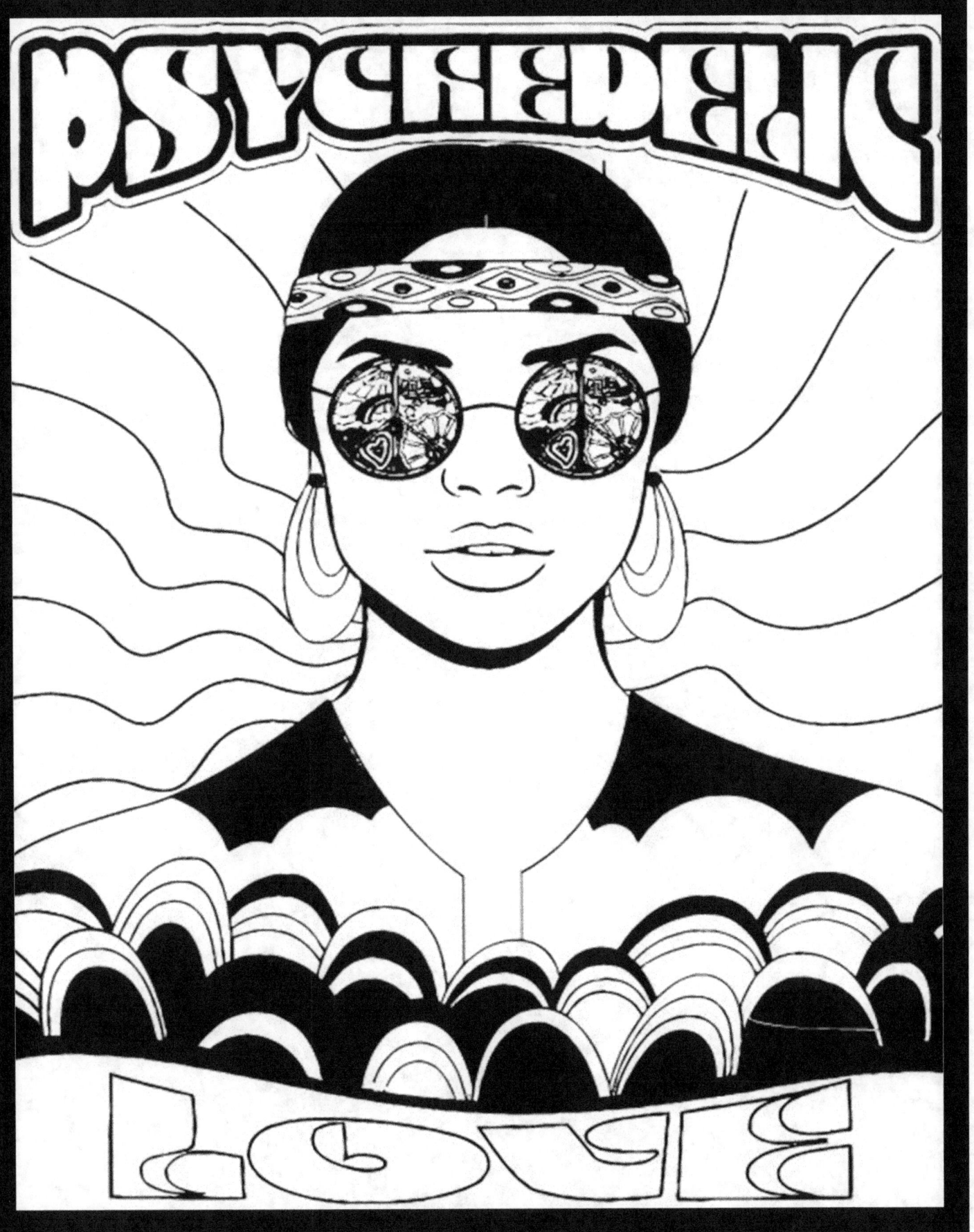

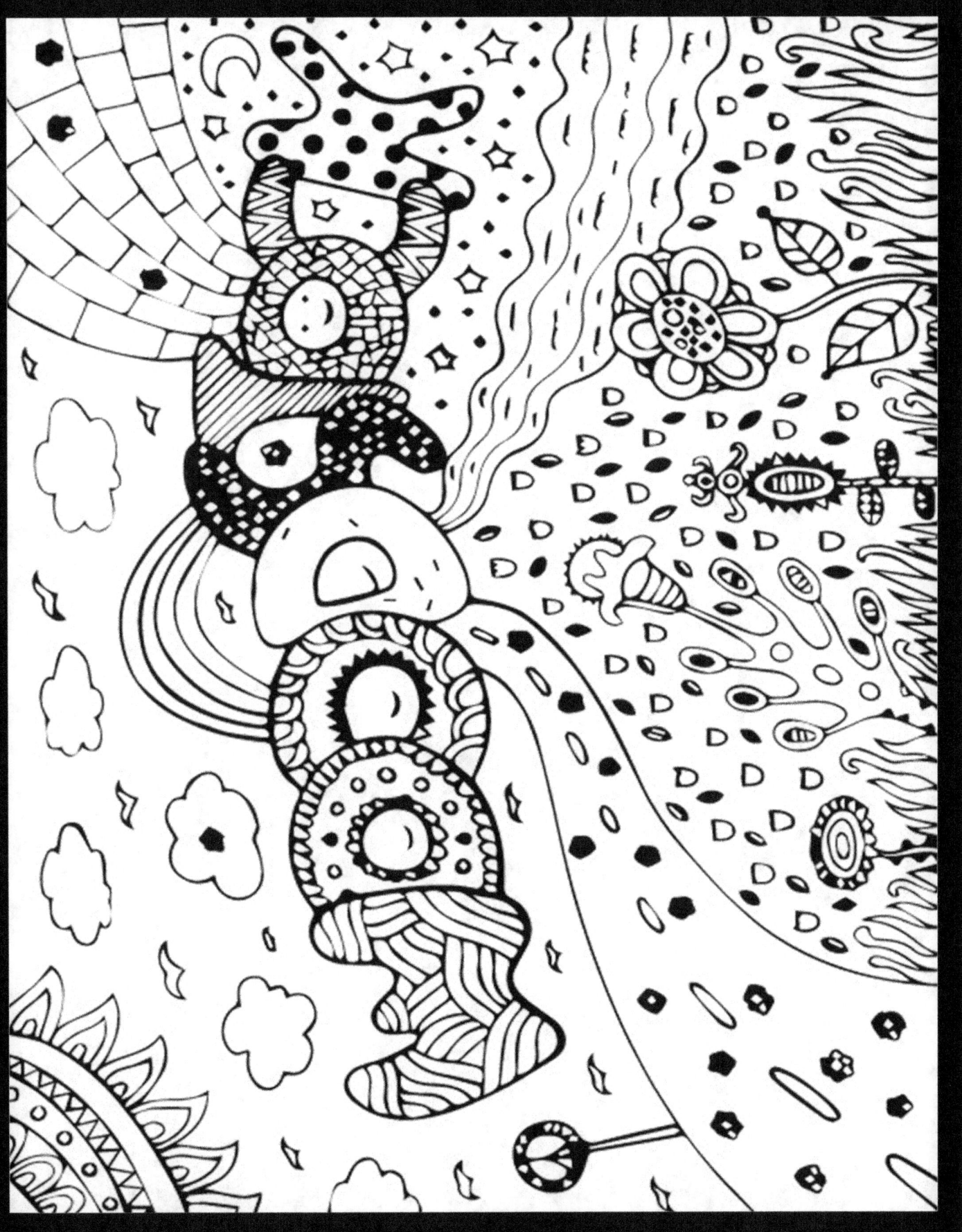

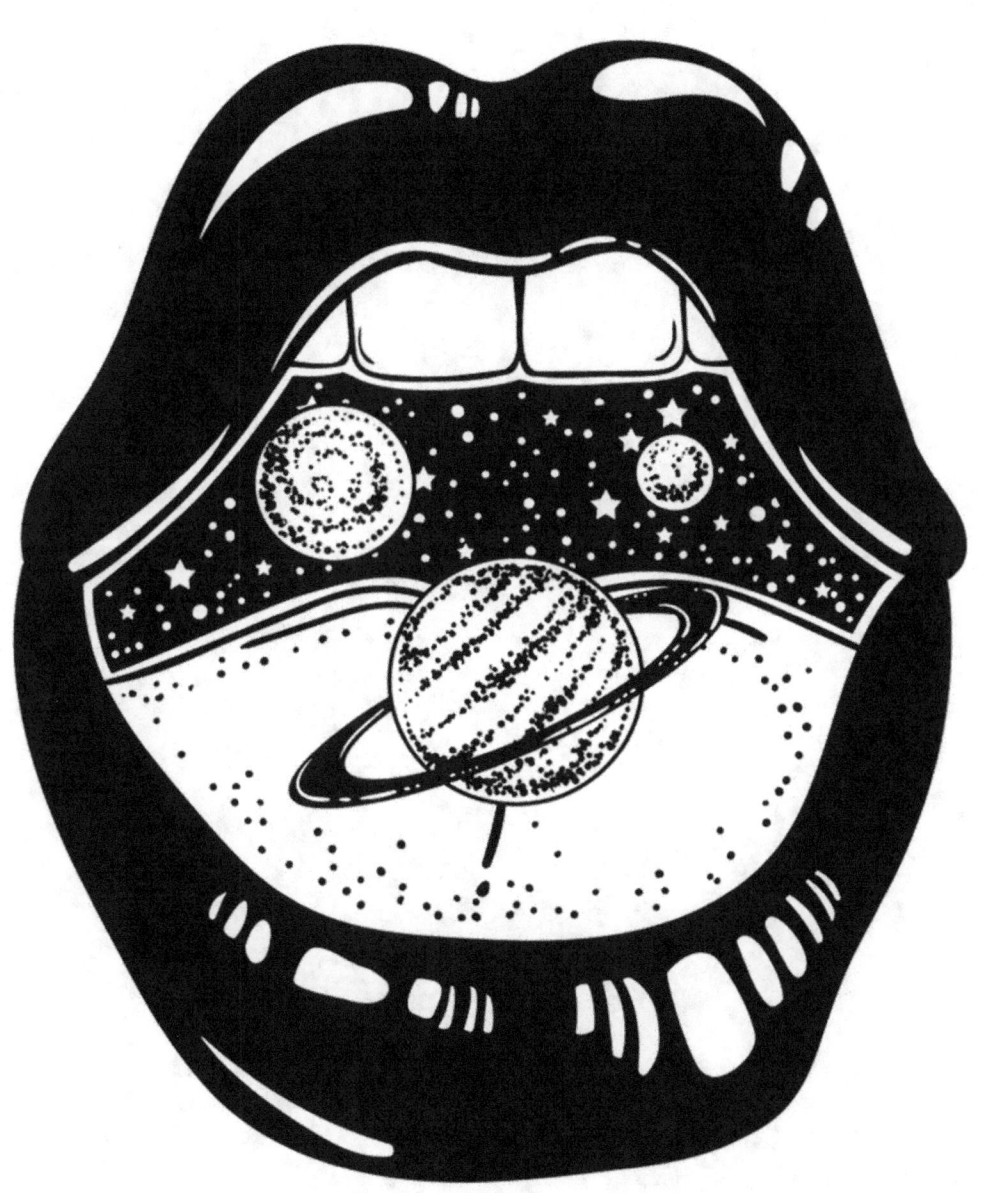

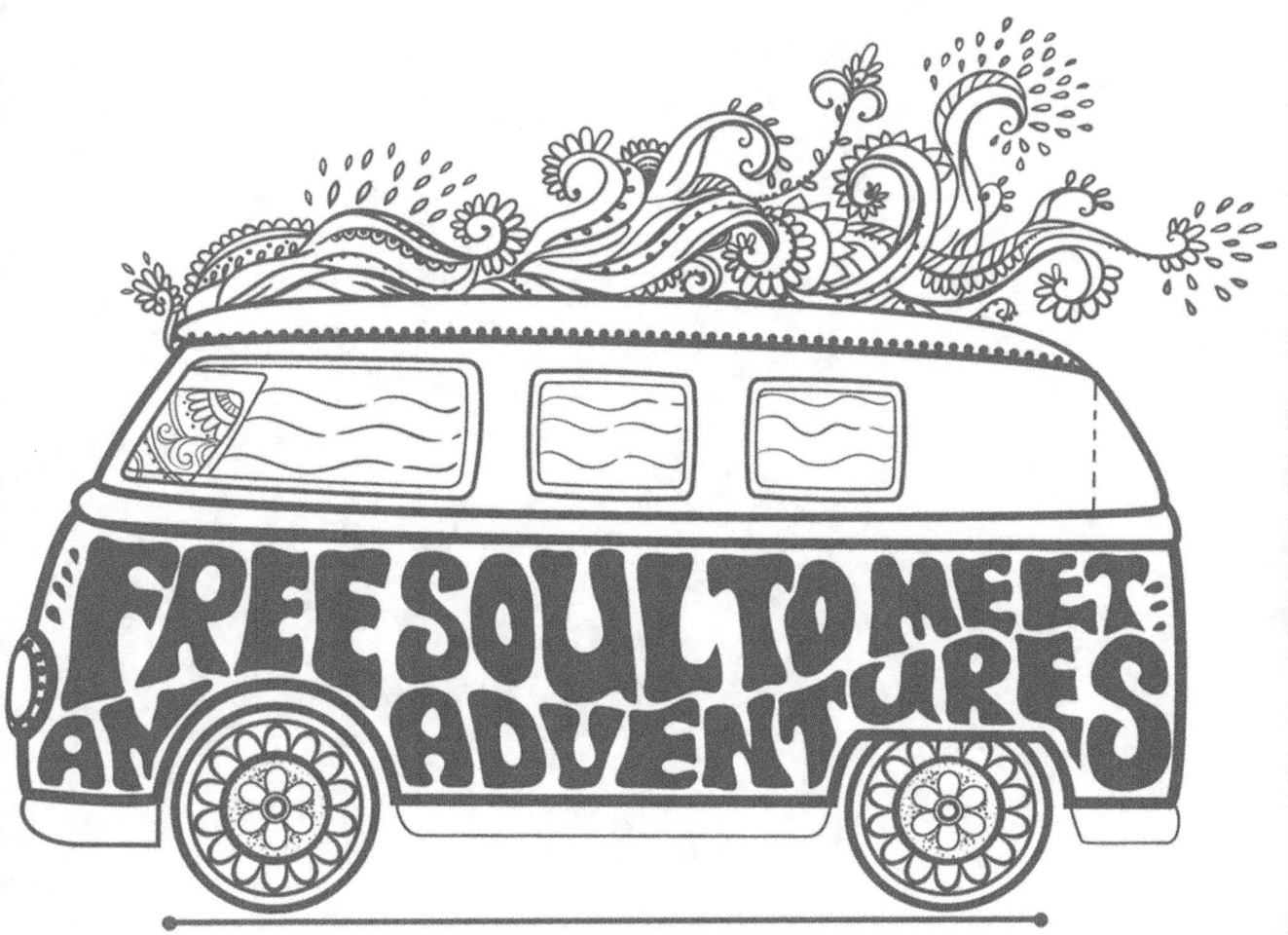

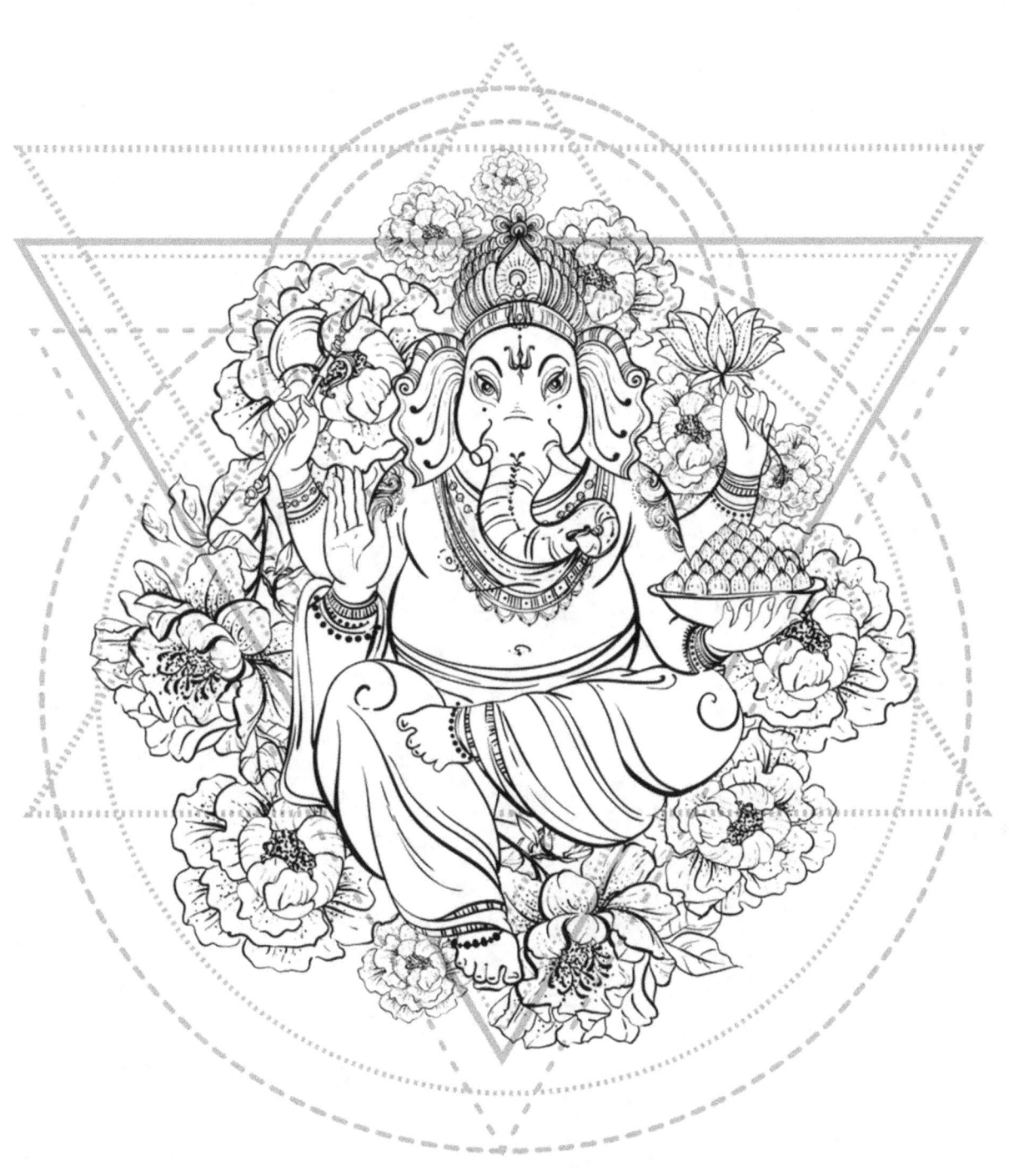

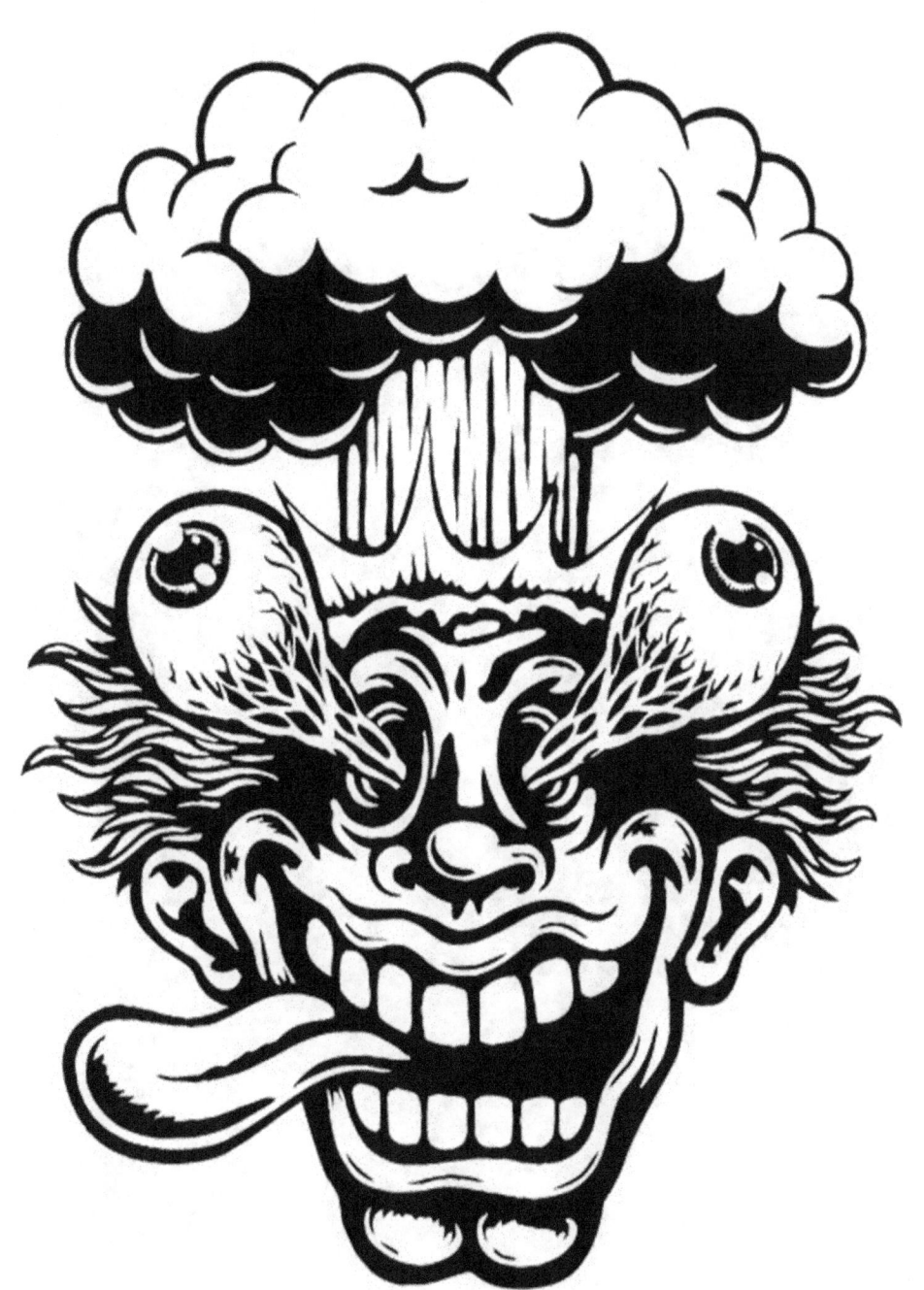

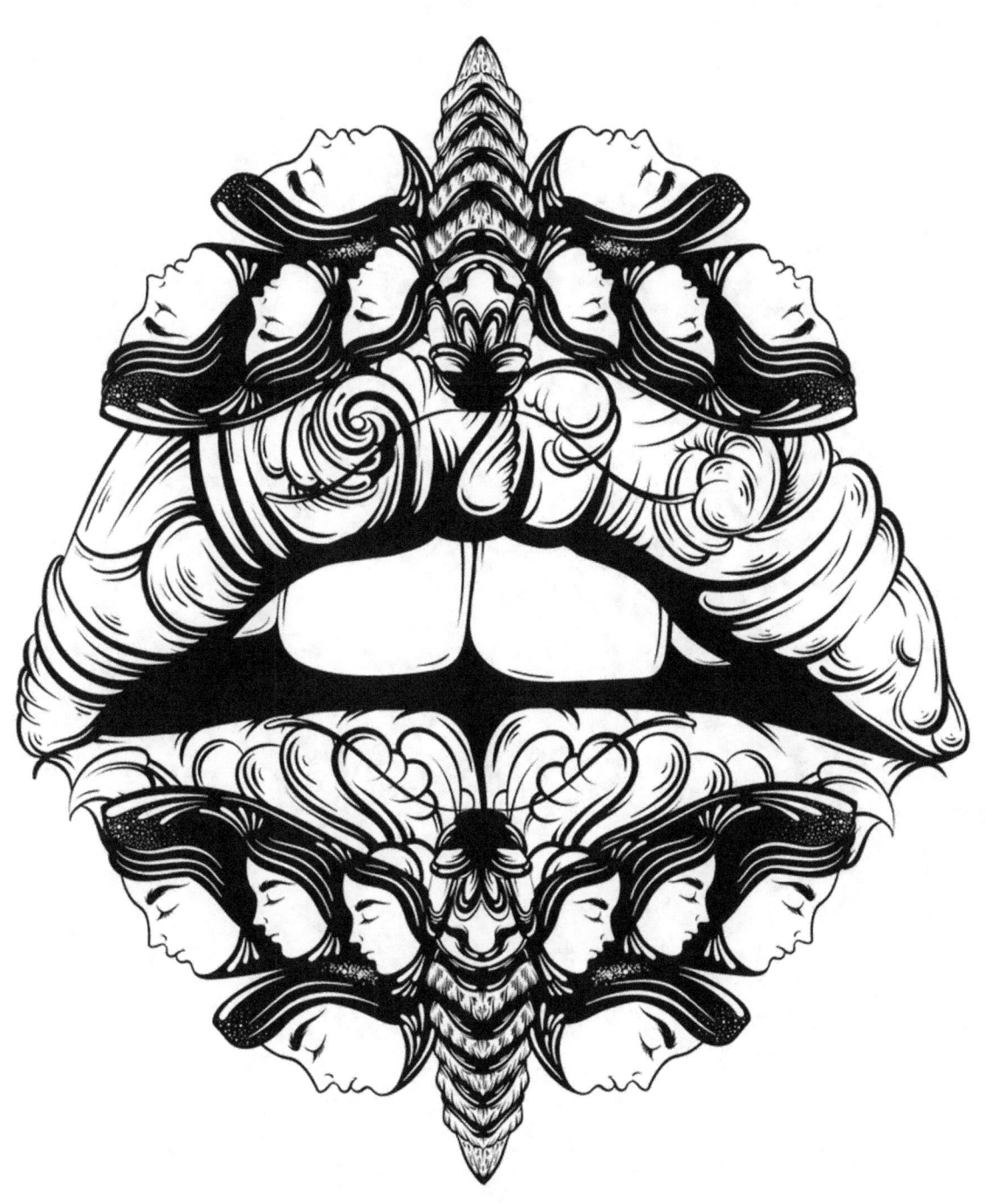

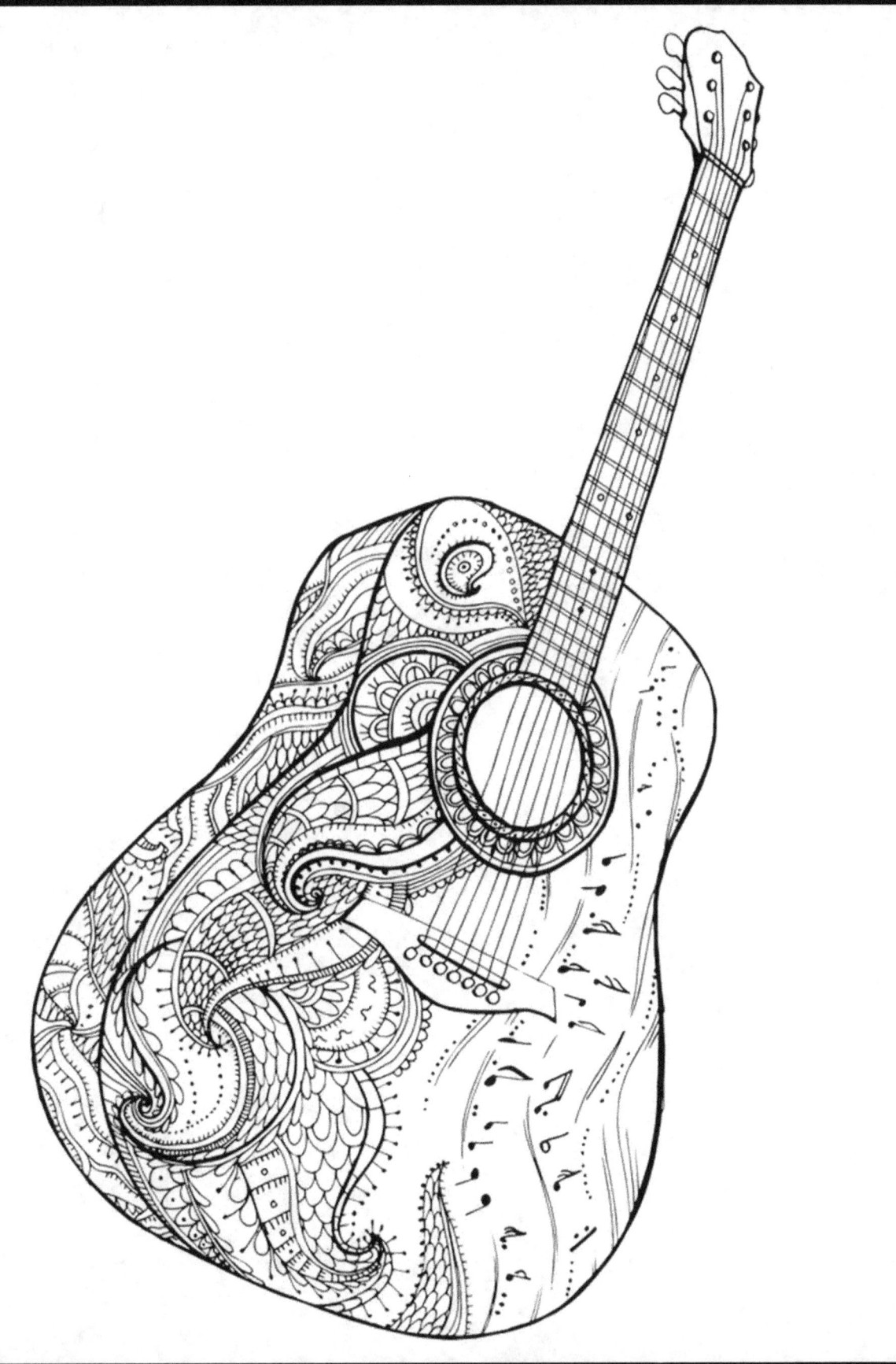

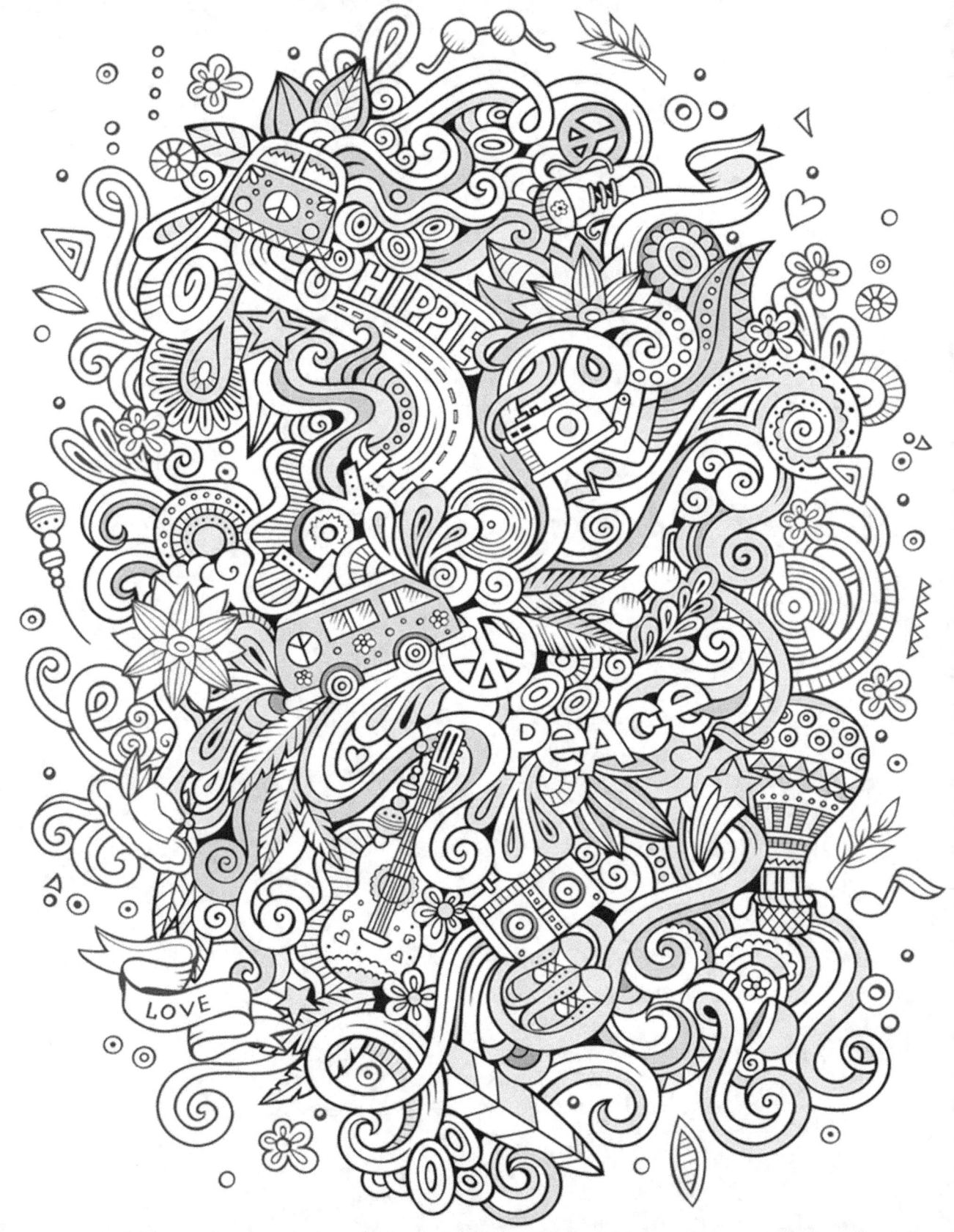

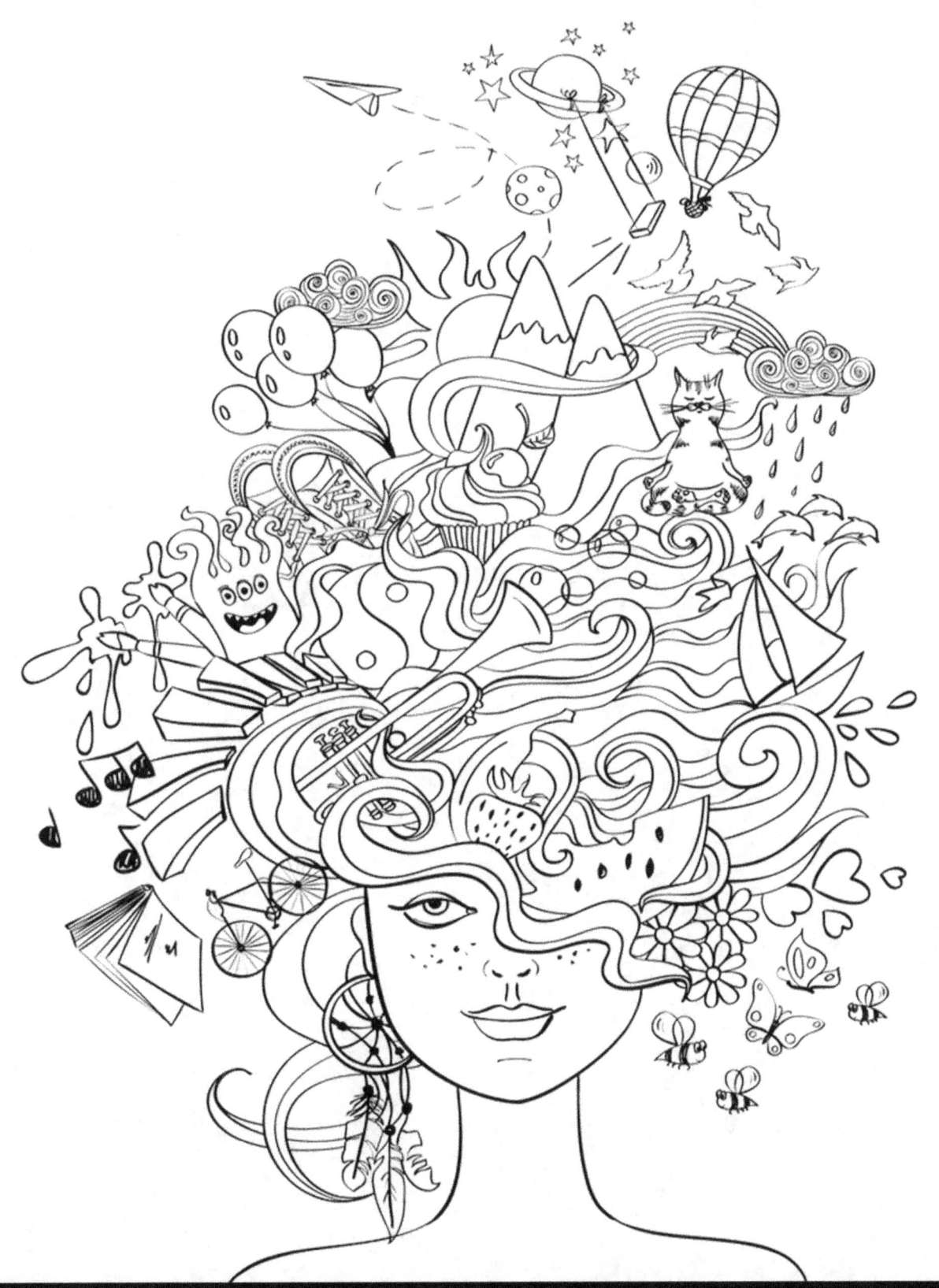

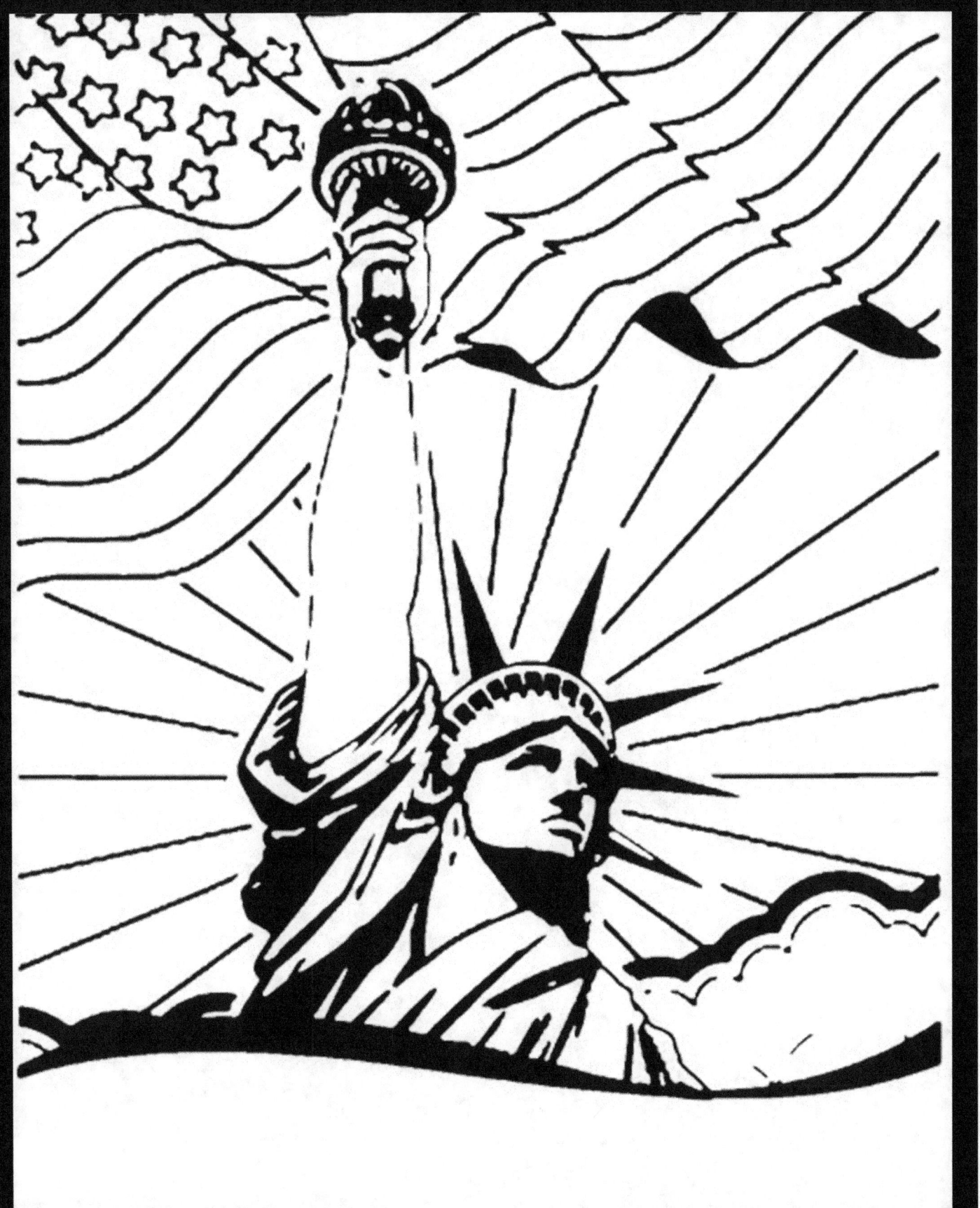

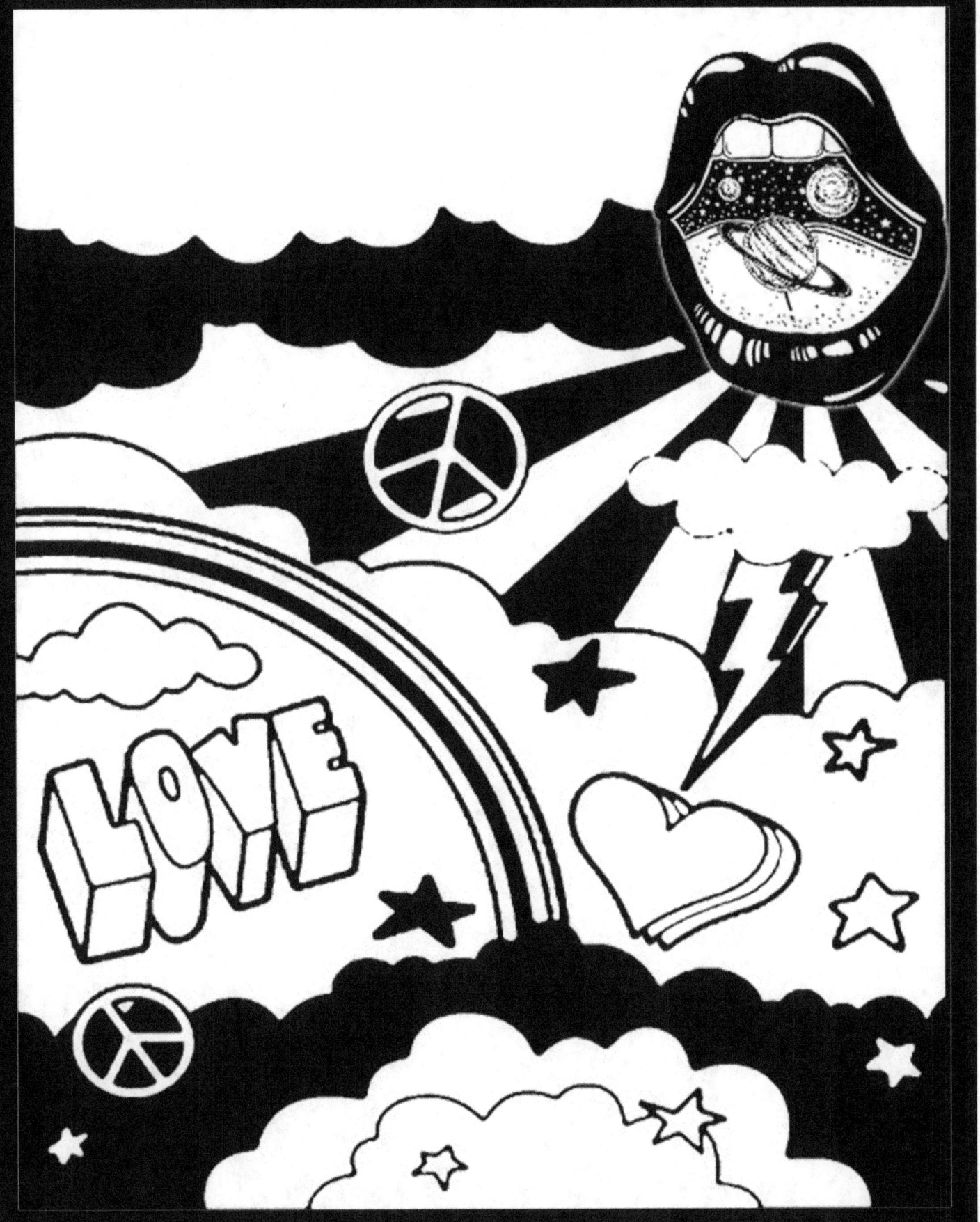

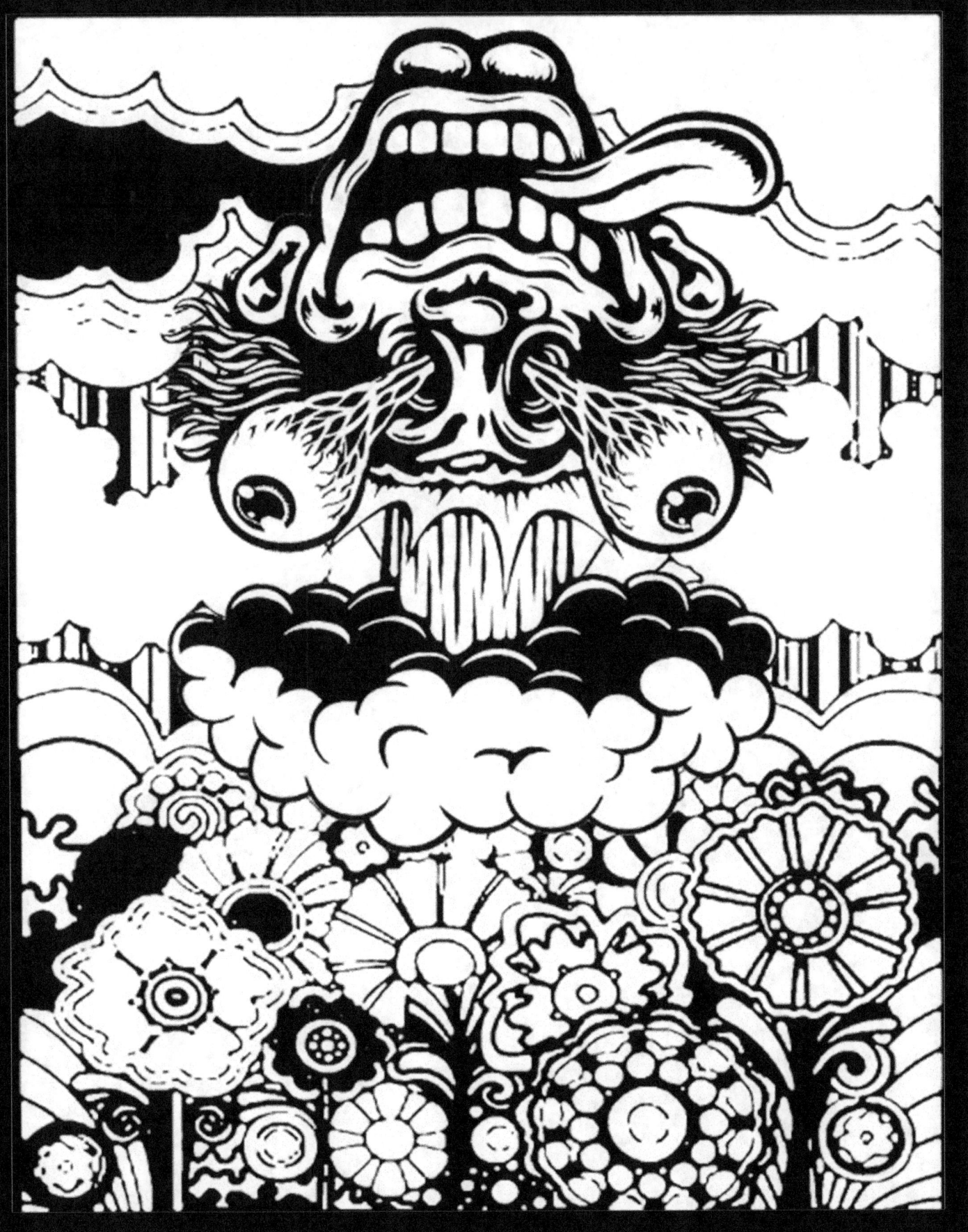

www.ingramcontent.com/pod-product-compliance
Lightning Source LLC
Chambersburg PA
CBHW080514220526
45465CB00006B/2486